THE NATURE OF DANCE

THE
NATURE OF DANCE

An Anthropological Perspective

RODERYK LANGE

INTERNATIONAL PUBLICATIONS SERVICE
NEW YORK

Published in 1976 by
International Publications Service
114 East 32nd Street
New York, N.Y. 10016

© Macdonald & Evans Ltd, 1975

Library of Congress Cataloging in Publication Data

Lange, Roderyk.
    The nature of dance.
    Bibliography: p.
    Includes index.
    1. Dancing—Philosophy. I. Title.
GV1588.L34   793.3'01   76-3471
ISBN 0-8002-0170-1

Printed in Great Britain by
Butler & Tanner Ltd
Frome and London

Preface

This book is intended to be an introduction to the problems of the development of dance in the context of human culture. A fuller understanding of the role dance has played throughout the different stages of the evolution of the human race must have a decisive meaning for anyone working contemporarily with dance, whether practically or theoretically.

There are indeed already many works on the history of dance. They present very elaborately the different facts, taken mainly from written sources. But even if they begin to explore the problem of dance origins and "primitive" dance, there is a feeling created in the reader that he is remote, distanced from it. The historical facts as they are presented in such books usually appear somehow alienated from our contemporary style of life, our needs in the modern world.

Dance anthropology, which is the subject of this book, on the contrary, deals with the unwritten sources of dance, with facts that are still alive among us today in remote places. Dance material is relatively conservative, and especially among cultures that are still highly integrated and have been relatively little disturbed, old patterns of dance prevail. They are the most reliable documents concerning the history of dance, and they can still be studied in the context of the way of life that gave rise to them.

It would be impossible to understand many facts in our contemporary life, not to mention making any attempt to shape a purposeful future, without trying to understand such a heritage from the past.

Man has become so very independent from his natural environment that he has taken some areas of his development into his own hands. Only a deep understanding of our faculties and their potential for development and growth can guarantee a satisfactory result in man's search for self-knowledge.

The appreciation of dance as a human faculty has for long been neglected. There are objective reasons for this, the main difficulty being that dance is with us only as long as we dance, only lasts as long as it is being performed and only has a significance in ourselves—as the human body is its only instrument—never becoming a material fact. Being so close to any dancing being, dance is difficult to investigate, one can rarely get far enough away from the experience to gain the necessary perspective. Far behind musicology and other studies in the humanities, choreology is only just coming to be accepted, only very slowly proving itself a valuable member among the other disciplines.

Rudolf Laban's greatly misunderstood explanations of human movement as having both physical and spiritual congruity form the "technology of dance," as opposed to dance technique. For the first time, things happening in the course of a dance have been given specific names, made apprehensible by his explanation and exploration of the range of human movement, and the extremes between which it always operates. This creates for the first time the possibility of making observations about human movement objectively comprehensible in terms of proportional arrangements. Laban's notation is a fundamental tool for choreology, and is now beginning to find general appreciation. Since it is based on movement principles, it gives a deep insight into the logical patterns of human movement.

Dance anthropology explains how these patterns find expression within the context of human life and its social background. It is amazing how rarely the knowledge of anthropology and the social sciences has so far been used as an aid towards the fuller understanding of our contemporary lives.

This book is an attempt to direct the student towards this field and show him dance from a new perspective. It is intended to be a sincere help in any dance studies and activities.

The actual origin of this book is connected directly with my teaching activities at the Nicolas Copernicus University, Toruń, Poland, 1965–67, and at the Laban Art of Movement Centre, Addlestone, Surrey, England, 1967–72. I have been lecturing on Dance Anthropology in both places, always combining theoretical sessions with extensive practical work on dance.

Many questions have continually arisen, telling me about the immediate needs of my students. The answers supplied over the years have established the core of this book. Therefore I would advise the reader to study the book right through in search for answers. The problems explained have been arranged, starting with the basic elements and successively showing their place in the complexity of the dance.

My personal approach to dance has changed basically after spending twelve years in research expeditions. All my previous ideas on dance, its relationship to human beings and its history collapsed when they were confronted by the facts of dance met in remote villages, somewhere in the Carpathian mountains or in forgotten places of rural Eastern Europe. One has had to bow to the human dignity still preserved in the old patterns of life, where Dance has always played a vital role in organising the whole of life.

There is nothing idealistic about this. However, we remote people, who have lost this balanced way of life centuries ago, tend to idealise the picture of ancient life conditions. That is how the image of the "noble savage" came into existence in the eighteenth century, only to be shattered by the findings of travellers and ethnographers throughout the nineteenth century. But the image itself did not become less human because of that. On the contrary—it became humanly comprehensible, and it has come to be realised that it enshrines all the really permanent human values which have to be integrated within ourselves if we are intending to remain human.

Les Bois,
December, 1973   Roderyk Lange

Acknowledgments

There have been so many people and institutions truly helpful to me in preparing this work that these acknowledgments are not a burden, a formal duty to be fulfilled, but a real pleasure, a chance to express my gratitude to all.

The necessary literature for writing this book has been made accessible to me by the Library of the Royal Anthropological Institute in London. I wish to thank the Librarian for her extremely helpful attitude and for the excellent service in dispatching the many book parcels to my home.

My sincere thanks must go to the Library of the Musée National des Arts et Traditions Populaires in Paris for patient help and hospitality during my stay there. Especially I would like to express my gratitude to Mlle. Mauriange from the Iconographic Department for the kind concern she showed to my work.

Similarly, I would like to express my thanks to the Archives at the Maison de UNESCO in Paris for help and for permission to include in my book several of their photographs (Plates 7, 11, 74).

I am most indebted to the Anthropology Department, University of Auckland, New Zealand (Miss Wendy Pond) for supplying excellent documentation and material concerning Polynesian Dance and for the kind permission to reproduce some of the photographs (Plates 75-79).

My sincere thanks must also go to my friend, Mme. Milica Ilijin from the Musicological Institute of the Academy of Sciences in Belgrade, for her generous help and permission to include some of the photographs (Plates 56, 63, 65, 66, 67).

I am most grateful to Mme. Dora Stratou, Director of the Greek Dance Theatre in Athens, for giving her wonderful photograph (Plate 57) for my book. This is her personal snapshot made during fieldwork, and I appreciate this gift profoundly.

Mrs. Janina Marcinek, M.A., Cieszyn, Poland, my former student, co-worker and friend, has supplied the photograph of the "trojok" from Silesia (Plate 85). With the help of her family she arranged a trip to the countryside to have this picture taken especially for my book. Many thanks for all the friendliness she showed.

Many thanks also to my former student and friend, Miss Jennifer Shennan, B.A., Auckland, for supplying me with much valuable material from Australia and Melanesia and especially for giving me information on the Maori dancing, particularly about the activity of the dance group Te Roopu Manutaki.

Our friends, Jacqueline and Jean Challet, Paris, have allowed me to talk to them about my book and Jean offered one of his splendid photographs (Plate 3) for inclusion. Many warm thanks.

Also, for being so ready to talk over the concept of my book I would like to thank Muriel Topaz and Jacob Druckman, New York, and Dr. Francine Lancelot, Paris.

My very special thanks must go to Mrs. Maria Drabecka, M.A., Warsaw, for reading the manuscript and for all her valuable comments.

Also for reading the manuscript I am most indebted to Prof. Gisela Reber, Folkwang Hochschule, Essen-Werden, to Miss Pat Woodall, B.A., London and to our Jersey friends Miss Eugénie Thompson, Miss Ray Axon, and Mrs. Alison Bertram, who have all given me splendid support in my work.

My sincere thanks must go to Miss Tricia Doherty, my former student, who has helped so much whilst functioning as my secretary, preparing and reading the typescript.

The doyen of British dance historians, Mr. Cyril W. Beaumont, has kindly allowed me to quote two excerpts from books he has translated and edited—Arbeau's *Orchesography* and Rameau's *The Dancing Master*. I would like to express my sincere thanks for this.

The Encyclopaedia Britannica has granted permission to quote several excerpts from dance entries from different editions, which has enriched the survey in Chapter 1. I am most grateful for this opportunity.

The generous gift of many splendid photographs (Plates

23, 24, 27–35, 69) donated for the book by Australia House in London made it possible to illustrate Aboriginal dancing in Australia. I am most indebted for this help.

The National Gallery in London has kindly allowed me to use the photograph of Botticelli's *Mystic Nativity* (Plate 58), and for this I would like to express my gratitude.

All the remaining photographs have been kindly supplied by the following photo-agencies in London: Barnabys Picture Library (Plates 1, 5, 6, 8, 9, 64, 68, 70, 80); Camera Press Ltd. (Plates 4, 10, 12–20, 22, 25, 26, 37–42, 44–48, 50, 53, 54, 59–61, 71–73, 77, 81, 84); Robert Harding Associates (Plates 43, 51, 52, 55); Paul Popper Ltd. (Plates 21, 36, 49).

My greatest debt of gratitude, however, is due to all those informants in the villages, who have given me their time and hospitality during my fieldwork, teaching me about all that dance can mean.

Many thanks must also go to all those friendly people who have given me their support in different times during my work.

I am also most indebted to my wife for giving me encouragement in her quiet way and to Anthony for understanding that the writing of this book was not an easy job for me.

Contents

Contents

List of Illustrations

Chapter 1

Dance and its Origin: Definitions and Opinions

It is not my intention to write another book on the "history" of dance. So many have already been written. Without knowing, however, how human thought developed in defining the nature of dance in our European civilisation, it would be impossible to comprehend the many facts that we are going to discuss in this book. For this reason, we shall review the different opinions on the origins and nature of dance that have been expressed over the centuries, picking out for our study those of the most importance and thus establishing a *historical perspective* for our further investigations.

Greek antiquity has left us two works on dance that still survive. The first is a work by Athenaeus (beginning of the third century A.D.), entitled *Deipnosophistai* (translated into English as "Authorities on Banquets"), which contains discussions by a number of illustrious people on different aspects of life. It also includes remarks on dance. Athenaeus complains that the dance is progressively deteriorating in Greece and illustrates this by quoting different authors who were already beginning to report on this sad event in the fourth century B.C. Dances of the Greek past showed much more activity, modesty, discipline and care of the whole body.

The second work is Lucian's (or Pseudo-Lucian's) dialogue *On Dance* (second century A.D.). This is a discussion between two friends, one being an enthusiast of dance and the other its enemy. This shows that already there was felt the necessity to defend the status of dance.

Lucian's dialogue is of more value to us, as it treats the problem exhaustively, and is an aesthetic and psychological analysis of the art of the dance. There are two statements which are particularly worthy of consideration, as they reveal an approach to dance which is characteristic of the Greek classical civilisation.

The first of these is a description of the essence of mimic dancing. This type of theatrical dance evolved in a period (about 22 B.C.) after the old, dignified choral dances of the drama had lost their importance.[1] Actually the activity of dancing in Greece had started to deteriorate a long time before, together with the successive decline of moral standards following the Peloponnesian war.[2] Lucian says here what a dancer should strive to achieve:

> "And, as the most material and important point of his art consists in the imitation and accurate representation even of the most invisible things, the highest ambition of the dancer must necessarily be, what Thucydides says in commendation of Pericles, 'to know what is fit, and be able clearly to express it to others.' By the latter I here mean (not, like the former, by words, but) by the most intelligible language of gestures."[3]

This sounds like a standard recommendation which, in respect of theatrical dance, is still relevant in our time. The second statement, appearing slightly earlier in the text, must be added here, as it reveals the particular type of dance that Lucian is really concerned with:

> "For in fact it is no longer ago than ... the reign of Augustus, that this art, in comparison of what it formerly was, has made such a great progress. Those motions were, in a manner, but the roots and rudiments of dancing; whereas I here speak of the flower and the fruits of it that are come to maturity, without troubling myself about what the thermaystris or the crane-dances* were, as having no analogy to the modern dance. Entirely for the same reason, therefore, and not from ignorance it is that I say nothing, for instance, of those phrygian dances performed at drinking-bouts, and [which] presuppose drunken dancers; of those violent and fatiguing leaps, to the shrill notes of a

---

* "When Theseus sailed back from Crete," says Plutarch in his life of that hero, "he landed at Delos, sacrificed to Apollo, dedicated to him a statue of Venus, which he had obtained from Ariadne, and concluded the ceremony with a festive dance, wherein he, with the young Athenians that accompanied him, imitated the intricate entrance and outlet of the labyrinth; a dance which is still in use among the Delians, and is called the crane-dance (geranos). ... Thermaystris was a very violent sort of dance, accompanied with exceeding high jumps, in which, ere the feet came to the ground, several capers were to be cut." Eustath. ad Odyss. viii. 264.[4]

piping-girl, which are still in practice with the common people in the country."

From this statement it is evident that Lucian expresses disregard for the dance of the common people and for dances of the Greek past, when people still commonly held dances on many important occasions.

Actually Plato (428–347 B.C.) in his *Laws*[5] had already made this distinction. Only the "noble kind of dancing" was approved of by him. Any kind of dance connected with certain rites of expiation and initiation showing traces of a Bacchic nature and of a lascivious character would be unfit for the citizens and should be disposed of and dismissed. There was no place in his scheme of city organization for actions of "ugly bodies and ugly ideas." Only the solemn movement of "beautiful bodies" was the type of dance one should be interested in.

Consequently, Plato would not have acknowledged a savage war-dance or hunting dance or rain-dance as art. According to him art had to contain an element of imitation, which should not copy a fact but induce in the viewer an experience; it must reproduce, re-enact an emotion.[6]

Following Plato's viewpoint on dance, Aristotle (384–322 B.C.) formulated a definition as follows:

"For as men, some through art and some through habit, imitate various objects by means of colour and figure and others, again, by voice; so, with respect to the arts abovementioned, rhythm, words, and melody are the different means by which, either singly or variously combined, they all produce their imitation ... In those of dance, rhythm alone, without melody [can be enough]; for there are dancers who, by rhythm applied to gesture, express manners, passions, and actions."[7]

The concept of dance as belonging to the imitative arts was going to influence European ideas on dance many times in future centuries.

From this, we can already see how remote we were at the very beginnings of European civilisation from the idea of dance as a spontaneous and commonly-known human manifestation. It had already by then become instead a well-defined and cultivated activity.[8]

There is one important point, however: the Greek civilisation made even this cultivated art of the dance commonly accessible to all its citizens. Especially in the more remote periods of Greek antiquity, dance had been an important part of religious ritual, drama, education, and recreation. Athenaeus still claimed in the third century A.D. that in the old times dances had been worthy of free men, and participation in them made men into better soldiers.[9]

Only later with the decline of Greek culture did dance become less and less respectable. It was then confined to entertainment and finally left to be performed by oriental slaves. This was even more relevant in Rome. Cicero's opinion gives convincing evidence of the low status of dancing at that time:

"Nobody dances, unless he is drunk or unbalanced mentally."[10]

The ancient Greek idea of "noble dancing" was, however, taken on by the rising European civilisation, together with many features inherited from Graeco-Roman antiquity. Considering how very much Christian thought was influenced by Plato directly or indirectly,[11] it is not surprising for us to find that the attitude to dance in early Medieval Europe had already been shaped in Antiquity. Thus dance was an important element in Christian-Gnostic mysticism in the third century, and was also accepted later by the official Church.

The "barbaric" peoples, nations newly converted to the Christian faith who had their old established cultures, and who often had not been included into the Roman Empire, took on the Christian civilisation very superficially. The new Christian ideology was simply a label, sometimes necessary for political or administrative reasons; indeed, many of the people either lived in areas too remote from the Church and administrative centres, or the conditions of their existence, despite their access to Christian Europe, were so little affected by it that the old structure of life still retained its validity. Thus the old "pagan" dance culture, being so much an integral part of their way of life, often prevailed with but slight modifications. Sometimes even in this day and age traces of it may be discovered as a secondary stream under the "European" surface,[12] as for example in some of the old peasant cultures, where dance plays a major role in magic rites and customs of family life, pastoral economy and the agricultural cycle.

Naturally, among these peoples there was no evidence of an understanding of the "noble" and refined "art of dance," as presented by Lucian. The Church preached intensively against the dance all through the Middle Ages: the "heathen" content of the common people's dances had too obvious a connection with the old ideology to be tolerated by the Church, which was trying to shape a new picture of Christian Europe.

However, in its own liturgy, the Church tried to maintain the "noble" form of dance as passed on by Antiquity, and because dance had already before been a part of the divine service and ritual, the young Christian Church had to retain it, whilst endeavouring to give it a new religious significance. Dance was described as one of the heavenly joys and as a part of the adoration of the divinity by the angels and by the saved.[13] In spite of the later "purifying" tendencies of the Church, which was a reaction to the fact that the "heathen" content overpowered the religious dance,[14] we can still witness today traces of dance actions surviving even in the liturgy of the Roman and especially in the Orthodox Churches.[15] Examples are the processional entry of the clergy, the hymn of the Cherubim, the gestures of the priest in prayer at the altar during mass. The dances that formed part of the old Spanish liturgy are still performed in the cathedrals of Seville and Toledo.

The movement of the Renaissance tried once again to return to the "classic" ideas of Graeco-Roman Antiquity.[16] The spirit of dance in the "official" European civilisation changed accordingly. Dance masters tried hard to follow what Lucian, Athenaeus and other Greek authors had written on dance. Domenico da Piacenza opens his codex on dance (mid-fifteenth century) by quoting Aristotle's opinion. After the condemnation of dance by the Church in the Middle Ages, it was necessary to justify the new affirmation of dance and to defend its moral value, by referring to Greek Antiquity's conception of "noble dancing" and also to the Holy Scriptures, where dance is mentioned in conjunction with religious service.

Thoinot Arbeau, in his treatise *Orchesography* (1589), says:

"For one who has spoken ill of dances, there are an infinity of others who have praised and esteemed them. The holy and royal prophet David danced before the Ark of the Lord. And as for the holy prophet Moses, he was not angered to witness dancing, but grieved because it was performed round a Golden Calf, which was idolatry. As for Cicero, he had swollen veins and limbs and traduced that which he could not perform himself, saying that he did not like to see people dance who were fasting. Appius Claudius, after a victory, approved dances. Indians worship the sun with dances. And those who have voyaged to newly discovered lands report that the savages dance when the sun appears on the horizon. Socrates learned dancing from Aspasia. The *Salii*, the very noble priests of Mars, danced at their sacrifices. The Corybants in Phrygia, the Lacedaemonians and the Cretans danced as they went against their foes. Vulcan engraved a dance on a shield ... a very beautiful object for the eye."[17]

This "classic" approach to official European dance was naturally confined to the court dance of that period; but anyway it had little in common with the dance of Antiquity itself. No matter how much dancing masters and authors of dance books (called codexes) referred to the classic period, it could only be to appeal to the idea of the "noble" way of dancing and not to the actual dance forms. The definition of dance, as presented by Lucian, still stood unchanged like a lonely pillar for a long time to come, as there was no further thought advanced on the idea of dance.

It needed the very strong personality of a Louis XIV (1638–1715) to give dance a new status. With Beauchamps as the main dancing master, Lully as the main composer and the King himself as the main dancer, dance became successively an obligatory part of a civilised man's way of life. This, however, was restricted to the royal court, to the "classic" revival in the palace of Versailles, in an artificial world circling around the King who declared himself to be its sun. The "pure" form of dance became the very means of expression of this formalised style. The allegoric stories of ballets were simply pretexts for displays of dancing. Technically, the form was relatively complex, as the King and the aristocratic courtiers concentrated on dance as one of their main activities,[18] naturally with the reservation that the King had to appear as the best performer of the court ballets.[19]

The patronage of the King over the art of dancing was most profound in its consequences. The direct participation of the King in dance and the establishment of the Academy of Dance (L'Academie Royale de Danse) in 1661 gave dance the merit of an official and respected art. Beauchamps established the rules of dancing, concentrating on the technique and polishing the abstract form. This conception of "pure" dance also found a theoretical support. In 1682, the Jesuit Father, Claude-François Ménestrier published the first history of dance, *Des Ballets Anciens et Modernes selon les Règles du Théâtre*, the high standard of which is still amazing today. In his period, the "three unities" (of time, place and action), were the basis of the classic French theatre, the rules of which were strictly followed; but, in respect of ballet, Ménestrier dared to deny them, claiming that dance was an independent art and had to follow its own particular rules. A ballet therefore should not be considered "a mute tragedy or dance comedy." At the same time, he was familiar with the ancient viewpoints on dance, and followed, for example, Aristotelian methods in analysing dance movements.[20]

After the King retired from performing in the court ballets (1669), the professional dancers took over, widening the scope of dancing and establishing successively over the next three centuries the tradition and style of the European brand of theatrical dance known as the "classical ballet."[21]

Louis' genuine contribution was appreciated by his contemporaries and by posterity. The dancing master Rameau, for example, gave him full acknowledgment in his book, *The Dancing Master* (1725):

> "The reign of Louis the Great will ever be regarded with justice as the epoch of the most illustrious men. Among all the arts which have flourished through the encouragement and liberality of so powerful a monarch, dancing has made the most rapid progress; everything has contributed to this end."[22]

This "classical" revival definitely established the position of dance as an art in modern Europe, but it was confined to the court circles of Europe and later to theatre performances, whereas in Greek Antiquity it had generally been acknowledged as a necessity in everyone's life. This has never occurred again in the history of European civilisation. Several times later people (Vigano, Blasis, Duncan) endeavoured to revive this Greek ideal of the dance, but it always proved to be a pale shadow of its original, remaining an illusion of the creators of these particular styles, who believed that they were truly dancing like the ancient Greeks. In reality, this could never be achieved. These "revivals" have been placed in a different period, far remote from Greek Antiquity, where common participation and understanding of dance as an art were evident. The conditions of life in modern Europe never again reached the humane standard of Ancient Greece.

The picture of dance in modern Europe would not, however, be complete if we omitted to mention Jean Georges Noverre (1727–1810), who also contributed fundamentally to the development of the European art of the dance. His famous *Letters on Dancing and Ballets* (1760) exercised a particularly profound influence on theatrical dance for a long time after his death, and changed the face of European ballet entirely again.

Noverre attacked L'Academie Royale de Danse for not having produced any new writings on the theory or practice of dance. He rose against mere empty virtuoso performance and demanded that the rigid schematic formulas in movements, steps and gestures, be dropped. His desire was that dance (on stage) should become a drama, picturing life (*danse d'action*), and that each of the dancer's movements should result out of the action and respond to motions of his soul (*mouvements de l'âme*). He also demanded that the dancer be educated and responsive. The "art of the dance" was for him a synthesis of music, painting and sculpture:

> "Poetry, painting and dancing, Sir, are, or should be, no other than a faithful likeness of beautiful nature."[23]

Noverre himself, being a self-taught man, was very conversant with literature, music and art. His correspondence with Voltaire is good evidence of this.[24] We also know that Noverre was enthusiastically involved in drama, and especially with the style of acting of the English actor David Garrick (1717–79).

The main principle in the approach that dance should "imitate" the beauty of nature goes back to the classic definition of Lucian. The term "imitate" in the eighteenth-century language of aesthetics indeed meant to create an imitation which would evoke in the spectator the impression of "movement," "affect," "agitation."

Actually, Noverre had spiritual support in some of the French encyclopaedists. Diderot, in his *Entretiens sur 'Le Fils Naturel'* (1757) said:

"The art of dance is bad everywhere because one does not suspect that she is the art of imitation."

Further there is the most remarkable statement:

"Dance, in fact is a poetry. And as such it should have its own means of expression."

The encyclopaedist, Louis de Cahusac, in his book *De la Danse Ancienne et Moderne* (1754), said that dance

"... is an imitation of nature through the medium of movement, an imitation postulating the competition between the poet, painter, musician and the mime."

He declared that dance belonged to dramatic art, and also introduced excerpts from Lucian's dialogue into his book. We know that Noverre read Cahusac's book and that he later quoted Lucian in his own letters.

Noverre widened the scope of the ancient idea of dance. Dance in the theatre became with him the "synthesis of music, poetry, painting and sculpture," transformed, however, to meet the modern European demands of his time. Being a ballet master himself, he carried out his ideas in his life, and he must have shocked audiences a great deal, as they were accustomed to expect only pleasant entertainment from dance. Although he was not generally appreciated by his contemporaries, Noverre succeeded in establishing dance on the modern European stage by raising its status to a level equal to that of drama.

It is interesting to trace the growth of ideas about dance in the compendia of modern knowledge produced from the eighteenth century onwards—the encyclopaedias. There is, for

example, a definition of dance in a short entry (p. 305) in the
first edition of the *Encyclopaedia Britannica* of 1768–71:

> "Dance, an agreeable motion of the body, adjusted by art
> to the measures or tune of instruments, or of the voice."

It stresses further that

> "Dancing is usually an effect and indication of joy."

It also admits that:

> "It has been in use among all nations, civilised and bar-
> barous [and] sometimes made an act of religion."

A most illuminating conclusion for us follows:

> "The Christians are not free from this superstition; for in
> popish countries certain festivals, particularly those of the
> Sacrament and passion of our Lord, are celebrated with
> dancing."

The entry on "Dance" or "Dancing" in the third edition of
the *Encyclopaedia Britannica* of 1788–97 (pp. 659–72) had
grown into a long article. The first sentence of the definition
on dance is repeated from the first edition, but then follows
an addition mirroring the interest in the classic revival of the
Enlightenment (Diderot, Cahusac, Noverre), as discussed
above: Dance may also be

> "... the art of expressing the sentiments of the mind, or
> the passions, by measured steps or bounds that are made
> in cadence by regulated motions of the body, and by graceful
> gestures; all performed to the sound of musical instruments
> or of the voice."

Further on, it states:

> "There is no account of the origin of the practice of danc-
> ing among mankind."

However, it confirms that all people know how to dance, and
that it must be based on the function of the human body. The
connection between certain sounds and

> "... motions of the human body called *dancing*, hath
> seldom or ever been inquired into by philosophers."

It further investigates the influence sounds must have on human beings as they even cause the walls to vibrate (!). Then an interesting statement follows:

"As barbarous people are observed to have the strongest passions, so they are also observed to be the most easily affected by sounds, and the most addicted to dancing."

There was, however, at that time a philosopher's investigation in progress into the problem of dance. This was made by the Scottish political economist and philosopher, Adam Smith (1723–90). In his *Essays on Philosophical Subjects* (published 1795), there is a treatise on the sciences and arts. In it is included an amazingly general and basic appreciation of dance which goes far beyond that "classic" attitude as adopted by the Enlightenment. Smith acknowledges music and dancing as the natural pleasures of man after he has fulfilled his "bodily appetites." In man's cultural development, Smith places dance and music as the

"... first and earliest pleasures of his own invention"

as opposed to man's biology, which is not controlled by him. Following that comes the conclusion that

"... no nation has yet been discovered so uncivilised as to be altogether without them [dance and music]."

Smith also points out that rhythm is the connecting principle between both music and dance, and he indicates social background as a factor in dance development.

Romanticism, being a reaction to the neo-classicism of the late eighteenth century, had already been preceded by an upsurge of sentimental ideas about "natural" life as created by Jean-Jacques Rousseau (1712–78). This led to a special type of interest in folklore and folk-song. It became fashionable to write poetry in the style of the idealised "folk." In conjunction with this, folk dances were adopted for the use of the "civilised world."

This had happened before; for example, we only need mention the French court dances such as the branle, bourrée, minuet and gavotte,[25] which all have their prototypes among the peasant dances. But Romanticism brought a new awareness of the special "natural" value of all things originating from the "folk." In some countries, it even became the vogue for the nobility to dress up as "peasants." This also resulted in the transference of some of the peasant dances to the ballet stage: Fanny Elssler (1810–84) and Maria Taglioni (1804–84) performed some "folk dances," with much approval from the audiences.

This originally sentimental approach gradually developed into a genuine interest in the art and life of the common people and peasants of Europe. Many collections of folk-songs were started from first-hand observations.

The later nineteenth century brought the awareness that this unknown and often humiliated secondary stream of culture was in reality the most genuine part of national heritage. Dance was included in these attempts to rescue the vanishing folk culture.

In 1893, Arthur Hazelius organised the Folk Dance Society in Stockholm (Svenska Folkdansens Vänner), and its activities resulted in the formation of the folk dance archives at the Nordiska Museet.[26] This example has been followed by the remaining Scandinavian countries,[27] with the establishment of places such as the open air museums in Sorgenfri near Copenhagen, or in Aboland, Finland (already in 1890). In Britain, work was started by Cecil Sharp (1911),[28] and in Germany by Anna Helms-Blasche (1925),[29] to mention only a few of the most important names and places.

The folk dance revival of the nineteenth and twentieth centuries naturally had local variants, and it would be impossible to generalise about its achievements. In most cases, however, it was not realised that the rural dances, once taken out of their original environment, did not retain their form and content. Used by people of a different social group and in different conditions, the dances' function changed, and consequently so did their form. If people danced no more for themselves, but for onlookers, the aspect of the dances changed correspondingly. They often simply became different dances, at least, in their expression.

Although this revival approach was misleading in many instances, the fact remains that the folk dance groups contributed enormously as an educational stimulus all over Europe. To people who had already been urbanised this gave a direct contact with rural dance, and also provided posterity with the first instructively written accounts of European peasant dance. Their value lay not in any sentimental attachment to "folk" but in the fact that these sources showed clearly that dance had been, not so long previously, an integral part of European peasant life, and that its role was comparable with that of dance among the "primitive" people. These sources tell us a lot about dance in our life in general.

The movement of Romanticism also brought changes to the theatrical art of the dance.[30] Noverre's and Vigano's models of *ballets d'action* were no longer fully acceptable as they abandoned the appreciation of pure form in dance. Romanticism brought the rediscovery of poetry in dance itself, revitalising the ballet after a period of stagnation. The poet Théophile Gautier (1811–72) contributed vastly to the outcome of the romantic ballet. He excelled not only in writing criticisms of ballets[31] performed at the Opéra, but he himself also wrote the most romantic ballet, *Giselle* (1841).

The expressive value of the abstract forms of the "classical ballet"[32] in themselves also continued to attract poets in a later period, for the romantic air in the art of ballet continued for a long time. Stéphane Mallarmé (1842–98) and Paul Valéry (1875–1945) were both enthusiastic about dance as an art form. It is also interesting to follow the parallels between Valéry's[33] viewpoint on dance and the philosophic concept of duration and movement as expounded by the philosopher Henri Bergson (1851–1941).[34] The apprehension of dance through intuition is followed in their approach, but at the same time the need for intellectual appreciation of a dance's theme is also stressed.

Herbert Spencer (1820–1903), the English philosopher, dealt with the problem of dance on several occasions in his writings. In the articles *On the Origin of Dancing* (1895) and *Dancer and Musician* (1895), he stated:

> "Muscular movements in general are originated by feelings in general"

and he described spontaneous dancing activity as the property of uncivilised or semi-civilised man, and contemporarily, children. From this Spencer tried to establish the development of dance, suggesting that there had been successively developing specialisations (ritual, religion, entertainment).

He also launched the theory of "surplus energy" as the reason for children and "primitive" man's spontaneous dancing,[35] (actually after F. Schiller). Spencer certainly shocked the Victorians with the idea that their well-behaved ballroom dances should be connected with the "wild peoples' prancing."

The ninth edition of the *Encyclopaedia Britannica* of 1875–89 (pp. 798–801) contained a shortened article on dance:

"Regarded as the outlet or expression of strong feeling, dancing does not require much discussion, for the general rule applies that such demonstrations for a time at least sustain and do not exhaust the flow of feeling."

Additionally, it states a little further on:

"But it is only in the advanced or volitional stage of dancing that we find developed the essential feature of *measure*, which has been said to consist in 'the alternation of stronger muscular contractions with weaker ones,' an alternation which, except in the cases of savages and children, is compounded with longer rises and falls in the degree of muscular excitement [after Spencer]. In analyzing the state of mind which this measured dancing produces, we must first of all allow for the pleasant glow of excitement caused by the excess of blood sent to the brain."

This article also contains Locke's statement:[36]

"... the effects of dancing are not confined to the body; it gives to children ... not mere outward gracefulness of motion, but manly thoughts and a becoming confidence."

The application of dance as a means of education by Froebel[37] is also mentioned, as well as its exploration in gymnastic movement (Jahn in Germany, Nachtegall in Denmark, Lewis in the U.S.A., Ling in Sweden). This is symptomatic of the nineteenth century: an awareness of the one-sided stresses created by urbanised conditions of life and the overpowering fact of industrial development had arisen. A reconstruction of conditions enabling the human body and mind to recover was desperately sought after.

It can be seen how the humanity studies advanced in the nineteenth century, acquiring some of the empirical methods from the natural sciences and taking advantage of anthropological data then at their disposal as never before.

A very important work appeared in 1896. It is, considering its time, a very well-founded presentation on work and rhythm, *Arbeit und Rhythmus*, by Karl Bücher, a German economist.

Bücher very convincingly shows, by means of examples from all over the world, how rhythm had been used to organise group activities. The unified rhythmic background had to be revealed to enable a group of people to perform their task in an organised way. Thus sounds and beats accompanying physical labours in many cultures contributed to the quantitative rise of end-products in work.

He also points out the inability of the "primitive" to distinguish between work and play, as well as his inability to withstand mental stress over a long period of time. One can also observe this trait in children. They rest as soon as they feel the need to do so.

However, in this book there are points which show distinctly how very lost Bücher became in many instances and how helplessly he tried to persuade the reader of the absolute supremacy of the Work ("Arbeit") in human life and history. According to him, all our activities are "Work," even those without any utilitarian purpose. Naturally, with this criterion, he arrives at questionable classifications (for example, tattooing, hair plaiting, performing circumcision, and even corporal punishment as performed by soldiers beating a delinquent, are work).

The second point in his presentation that causes difficulty is his idea of "rhythm." He estimates as the highest achievement in the line of rhythmic developments the narrow limit of metronomic-automatic type of time order. Bücher also avoids the problem of dance to the extent that this word does not even appear in the very detailed list of contents.

He wants to idolise work and therefore postulates, for example, that in most cases the songs that came into existence out of working activities initially became dance and cult songs, and then later were acquired as generally known folk-songs.

I wonder if one could ever perform any work to some of the intricate dance rhythms? But on top of that Bücher says himself that dance rhythms are something that arise out of *human creativity*, whereas during work, rhythms are conditioned by our bodily constitution and technical means used. How could he so decidedly follow this up by a statement (after the Italian author E. Ferrero) that dance does not require such an effort of thought and will as work?

All these misconceptions arise from the fact that he does not distinguish between the difference in *function* of work and poetry. He wants to see work, music and poetry as a unity. But there are countless examples in his very own book that show clearly that dance achieves a very sophisticated level as an art with some "primitive" peoples, who at the same time have not developed much of their technical equipment. This means that there is not necessarily a direct parallel to be drawn between the growth of art in human culture and technology.

Additionally, there is no connection made in Bücher's book with the spiritual element in creativity, nor is the magico-religious complex introduced as the driving force behind the outcome of many non-utilitarian activities.

What Bücher really wanted to establish was a common denominator for all human actions, and that was to be *human movement*. For this discovery, however, we have still had to wait for some time.

Opinions issued on dance at that time also became evident in the further development of the human sciences. Works dealing with the psychology of art and the history of culture were faced with the necessity of including at least a few sentences on dance, but the texture of dance is so elusive for many writers that one has the feeling they were trying to go around the problem rather than solve it.

However, there are also some well-orientated ideas on dance to be found in some works. For example, E. Grosse, in his *Die Anfänge der Kunst* (1894), set forth the high social significance of the dance. According to him, dance has contributed to social unification and social solidarity. Dance imparted courage and prepared people for war. All advanced civilisation is based on dancing. Dance has socialised man.

B. H. Schurtz, in his *Urgeschichte der Kultur* (1900), follows up what Bücher says about rhythm and work. But he states also that dance is the poetry of bodily motions and stresses its importance in human culture. According to Schurtz, dance originated as the outlet of joy accumulated within a group.

W. Wundt, in his *Völkerpsychologie* (1900–21), tries to

Plate 1 (*above*): prehistoric paintings done with bat guano, Magoura Caves, Northern Bulgaria.
Photo: E. Preston

Plate 2 (*right*): old Slavic idol, "Świato-wid," Ukraine. A closed circle of figures runs around the pillar.

Plate 3 (*above*): Bogomil tombstone, Brotujice, Dalmatia.
Photo: J. Challet
Plate 4 (*below*): the mating dance of cranes.
Photo: I. Linde

Plate 5 (*left*): a child in play.
Photo: A. Brims

Plate 6 (*right*): a spontaneous dance.
Photo: Hedgecoth Photographers

Plate 7 (*above*): children dance, Strba,
Slovakia, 1962.
Photo: UNESCO/A. Tessore
Plate 8 (*below*): children make music.
Photo: R. Engh

Plate 9: a dancer from the Dinka tribe, Southern Sudan.
Photo: M. M. Ninan

te 10 (*left*): dancing
ilst awaiting dignitaries,
inea.

Plate 11 (*above*): gathering for a festival, La Huachaca, Bolivia, 1971.
Photo: UNESCO/Zevaco

Plate 12 (*below*): a small boy dances during the witch-doctor's healing ritual, central Ghana.
Photo: J. Moss

Plate 13 (*left*): a young girl caught in a trance whilst undergoing therapy from her local witch-doctor, central Ghana.
Photo: J. Moss

Plate 14 (*left*): the "Twist," Brussels.
Photo: G. Nielsen

Plate 15 (*right*): a New York disco-
thèque.
Photo: B. Glinn
Plate 16 (*below*): a discothèque,
Dallas.
Photo: B. Glinn

Plate 17 (*left*): a young girl moves in a ritual dance. Karaja
Indians, Brazil.
Photo: R. Hanbury-Tenison
Plate 18 (*above*): Karaja Indian witch-doctors dance
under fearsome straw coverings, Brazil.
Photo: R. Hanbury-Tenison

Plate 19 (*above*) the girl meets witch-doctors in a ritual dance.
Photo: R. Hanbury-Tenison

Plate 20 (*above*): dance in the Voodoo cult, involving the invocation of a spirit, Haiti.
Photo: G. Mangold
Plate 21 (*below*): the fire-walking ceremony, Fiji Islands. The dancers step barefoot on red-hot stones, whilst an appeal is made to the tribal god.

Plate 22 (*above*): dances to attract forces of good intent, to placate evil spirits, to ensure the prosperity of the tribe, Africa.

Photo: P. Almasy

Plate 23 (*above right*): Australian Aborigines dance the myth of creation at the circumcision ceremony of the tribe's younger boys, Arnhem Land.

Photo: Australian News and Information Bureau

Plate 24 (*below right*): Aboriginal dancer, Darwin, Australia.

Photo: M. Jensen, Australian Information Service

establish some sort of provenance for dance based on the then accumulating descriptions of "primitive" peoples. According to his very artificially thought-out scheme of development:

> "One stream of Dance came into existence as an expression of personal feeling, mainly of 'ecstatic' character, and afterwards was secularised becoming 'social' dance, as a means to express joy and eroticism. A second stream of Dance came from magic ceremonies and cults[38] and can be described as 'dance in society,' with ordered and disciplined forms. From this stream of dance, mime also developed." (Vol. III)

But he gives in the same work a very convincing appreciation of dance as an art among the "primitive" peoples:

> "Not the epic song, but the dance, accompanied by a monotonous and often meaningless song, constitutes everywhere the most primitive, and in spite of that primitiveness, the most highly developed art. Whether as a ritual dance, or as a pure emotional expression of the joy in rhythmic bodily movement, it rules the life of primitive men to such a degree that all other forms of art are subordinate to it." (Vol. I, Part 1)

However, at that time we also come across more general and convincing formulations concerning the nature of dance. For example, the tenth edition of the *Encyclopaedia Britannica*, 1902–03 (pp. 372–77) contains a long article on dance by Alexander Bell Filson Young. Dancing is defined here as

> "... the universal human expression, by movements of the limbs and body, of a sense of rhythm which is implanted among the primitive instincts of the animal world."

In the eleventh edition of the *Encyclopaedia Britannica* of 1910 (pp. 794–800), however, the article on dance (Filson Young and W. C. H. Smith) brings, in addition to the previous concise statement, a discussion of different types of dancing which is not really helpful in getting to the root of things.

In 1913, Jane Harrison's *Ancient Art and Ritual* appeared. She decidedly refuses to call art any dance activities connected with fertility rites (p. 32) or magical dances because they are performed for practical reasons (!). According to Harrison's classification, these dances are not yet rituals, and it is only after they become rituals that they may then contain an element of imitation, thus giving them the status of art. Then only are they performed for an emotional end. It is clear that Plato's idea about the "noble dance" has been followed by this author very strictly.

Anthropology, in its rapid development, brought much insight into the nature of dance as a result of direct observation of the "natives." Some of the leading anthropological works of that period contained data and formulations on dance, *e.g.* E. B. Tylor: *Primitive Culture* (1871); *Anthropology* (1881), especially Chapter 12; O. Peschel: *Völkerkunde* (1874); F. Ratzel: *Völkerkunde* (1885–88). G. Buschan's *Neue Beiträge zur Menschen- und Völkerkunde* (1927) contains a statement on dance which is worthy of being mentioned here. He concludes that, of the musical arts, dance plays the biggest role among the "primitive" peoples.

The ethnographic literature of that period is full of verbal descriptions of dances from all over the world, but they are mainly mentioned only in conjunction with customs and music. Additionally, dances appeared to many of the authors of that time as very "exotic," "wild" and "indecent," and they were sometimes explained as manifestations of lower developed peoples. The "civilised" observers themselves would never have dreamt of performing such kinds of uninhibited movement.

In 1923, Havelock Ellis published *The Dance of Life*. Chapter 2 of this book is devoted to the art of dancing, and it is the most remarkable statement. The presence of the religious and erotic aspects of dance are stressed as simultaneous factors. Animal and primitive dance, he said, contain the element of sexual selection. Art in dance was already visible in courtship activities. Successively a specialisation had evolved, leading to dance as a profession where it might still retain a religious or ritualistic significance to varying degrees (medicine man, priest, ballerina). Two opposing patterns of life, urbanisation and ruralisation, had shaped the picture of dance. Urbanisation had eliminated the sexual message of dance.

"Morality, grown insolent, sought to crush its own parent, and for a time succeeded only too well." (p. 65)

Ellis also indicates that as a result of dance being a balancing and socially initiating factor in a child's development, it was desperately sought after as a means of education at the turn of the century.

The statement Havelock Ellis made about the balanced contribution of human biology and man's spiritual achievement to dance was absolutely epoch-making. With it Ellis vindicated for dance all that had been discarded since Plato's formulation concerning the superior value of "noble dancing" alone. However, it was all too much in advance of current thought to be recognised and accepted contemporarily. Actually Ellis' other monumental work, *Studies in the Psychology of Sex*, containing also a very fundamental contribution to the understanding of the nature of dance, resulted in legal proceedings being brought against him on grounds of indecency. The book itself was, until 1935, legally available for the medical profession only.

Ellis' books have been followed by an anthropologist's account on dance. In 1926 W. D. Hambly's *Tribal Dancing and Social Development* appeared. In spite of muddled criteria this work stresses clearly the importance of dance as a means of social organisation among the "primitive" peoples.

The advancement of interest in anthropology, psychology and the history of culture, so very significant in that period, was reflected to some extent in the different books on history of dance which were published in the 1920s. At least some attempt had to be made to define dance in them and to refer to its origin. Here are a few of these definitions:

"Dance originates from emotional impulse and improvisation." (Max v. Boehn, *Der Tanz*, Berlin, 1925)

"Dance came from the need to release psychic tensions by means of rhythmic movement." (Dr. J. Schikowski, *Geschichte des Tanzes*, Berlin, 1926)

"Dance originates from ecstasy ('individual,' formless) or from magic (determined and ordered forms). The dance form consists of movement shape, floor pattern and rhythm." (F. Böhme, *Massstäbe zu einer Geschichte der Tanzkunst*, Breslau, 1927)

The fourteenth edition of the *Encyclopaedia Britannica* (1929) (pp. 13–24), contains several articles under the entry

"Dance." The first of them (by Camilla H. Wedgwood, anthropologist and sociologist), opens with the following statement:

> "Dancing consists in the rhythmical movement of any or all parts of the body in accordance with some scheme of individual or concerted action which is expressive of emotions or ideas ... ."

This excellent modern definition is followed up by an ardent defence of "primitive" dancing which, at that time, was still being accused of being obscene because it was primarily sexual in intent.

In 1933, Curt Sachs published his *Eine Weltgeschichte des Tanzes* (*World History of the Dance*).[39] It was undoubtedly the first modern specialist study on dance based on material gathered from a vast area. Sachs, being a musicologist himself, applies methods of investigation which were well established in his own discipline and in the human sciences in general at that time. He analyses comparatively a great deal of the data on dance collected accidentally by ethnographers, and he tries to establish typologies for dance. In many instances he confined himself to discussing the different processes evident in dance, often reconstructing these in the course of an intellectual exercise from the material collected, which was never sufficiently complete. He often failed to identify the congruity of the various dance manifestations in their life context; but Sachs was not a dancer himself, therefore his criteria concerning forms and functions of dance were often too mechanistic. As a result, his survey lacks clarity, and many types of dance are intermingled and do not contribute to the picture of dance as a whole.

Sachs' typology was not based on any evidence resulting clearly from the analysis of dance materials. He instead imposed criteria (for example, those arising from Jungian psychology—introvert/extrovert). Sachs admitted the inadequate state of source materials for dance, and hence his desperate attempt to introduce criteria from these external disciplines.

But Sachs did offer solutions in his book which open the doors to a new understanding of dance. Firstly, he defines dance as rhythmical movement without stressing any utilitarian aspect (p. 6), ("Tanz jede rhythmische Bewegung, die nicht dem Werkantrieb dient"—dance is any rhythmic movement which does not serve the ends of labour), (p. 3, German ed.). Secondly, he states that dance as an art is basic and prior to any other creative expression in man, as the dancer uses his own body. The work and the creator are contained in the same person before other substance, for example, stone, canvas, word, sound, places itself between the artist and his inner experience (p. 3). Thirdly, as a result of his historical analysis, he points out that already in the Stone Age dancing had become art. It was only then, with the advent of the Metal Ages, that myth took over and raised dance to the status of drama; but as soon as dance became "art" in the narrower sense and started to serve man instead of spirits, it was degraded to a spectacle and its all-embracing power was broken. It split. The different components of dance emancipated themselves and became separate activities and arts such as games, physical exercises, drama and religions (p. 6).

It is characteristic that most of the published formulations on dance talk around this problem rather than delving straight into it. The most basic element of dance has been omitted from them all: namely, *human movement*. It is just as if one were to speak about music and to avoid entirely referring to its texture and basic material, sound.

This inability to approach dance in a more objective way is explicable, as it was only recently that a satisfactory concept of the structure and principles of human movement were put forward by Rudolf Laban.[40]

Laban started as a practitioner in dance and was in no way conventional. His new way of approaching dance on the European stage in the 1920s and 1930s brought about a most inspiring result. He tried to establish a system of dance following the breakthrough caused by the revolutionary Isadora Duncan. (Revolutionaries are not builders!) His achievements in that area are comparable to those of Noverre's in his time, whose great admirer Laban was himself.

However, Laban neither stopped at the classic Greek approach to dance as presented by Lucian (the division of dance into "noble art" and "savage" dance), nor at its application in the eighteenth century by the movement of the Enlightenment (synthesis of music, poetry, painting and sculpture).

He went far further, looking for a universal solution and a common application of dance in modern times,[41] and indeed, he turned to movement as the common denominator of all our actions, including our capacity to express ourselves as living beings.

Laban also parted from the conception of music as an inevitable element of a dance composition. This was an important attempt to liberate dance from the label of belonging to the "musical arts."[42] He created, as a result, several ballets without any music.

Laban was not a trained scholar.[43] Being an artist and a dancer himself, he was a good observer and had an ingenious ability to see the connections between dance in human life and in culture. Therefore it is not unusual that his contribution to dance and movement theory proved exceedingly relevant, and the movement theory he proposed, in its concrete practical evidence, made possible a great advance in the whole area of studies on dance. Despite many misunderstandings, Laban's concept cannot be dismissed, simply because no better solutions have ever been offered. His proposals open possibilities for further investigation in this very little known area of studies.

In his theory of movement, Laban's approach is entirely empirical. The scales and models he drew up are universally applicable in identifying any human movement in space, but naturally they serve only as a means of reference. It is, therefore, a misconception to confine this system to any specific philosophic or pseudo-philosophic trends, or to mechanically performed structures and exercises. Scales and harmonic structures are not yet dance in themselves. It is up to the mover, the dancer, to choose what kind of convictions he is following in *interpreting* the manifestations of human mind and spirit, as perceivable through dance.[44]

Laban himself, as an artist, was not free from the symbolic and mystic trends *of his time.* This is understandable as he was a creative artist himself and nobody is ever free from the influence of the artistic ideas current in their own time. However, this aspect of his work should not be confused with his contribution to the universally applicable theory of movement.

Laban followed up what the French artist François Delsarte (1811–71) had already established in his system of identifying movement expression.[45] He was also influenced by the contemporary results of anthropological and psychological research which were then developing so rapidly. Taylor's system,[46] also, with its motion studies, was drawing attention to the importance of precise knowledge about people's movement range. Primarily, however, Laban was a dancer, and was profoundly impressed by dance in the form in which it was still alive amongst people in the villages of Eastern Europe[47] where he spent his adolescence.

Laban's movement theory was presented as early as 1926, in his book *Choreographie*, but he only arrived at the final solutions after coming to England in 1937, when he concentrated mainly on the study of human movement.[48] These solutions are astounding. The discovery of models (dynamic structures) of human movement possibilities in space and time allows the proportional arrangements of qualities, evident in movement and dance, to be identified in an objective way for the first time. It is the *technology* of dance that Laban established, as opposed to *technique*. We are now able accurately to name the observable manifestations in dance. Through Laban, we have obtained a vocabulary for the study of movement.

Through these solutions, the first modern results in dance research are being achieved, for example, the works on structural analysis as performed by the Hungarian Academy of Sciences, or by the Dance Section of the International Folk Music Council, or the dance research as established for example in Poland and Yugoslavia.[49] The controversial cantometrics project at Columbia University, New York, also included an investigation into the cultural significance of dance,[50] where Laban's concepts have been applied.

A badly needed contribution in identifying the essence of dance, and concerning its meaning, has come in recent decades from philosophers and aestheticians and new valuable contributions to dance research have been worked out. Ernst Cassirer[51] and especially Susanne Langer[52] have put forward many clarifying statements. Also an exceptionally clearly laid out concept of dance has recently been presented by Maxine Sheets[53] in the light of phenomenological philosophy.

There are, however, certainly many problems which have not yet been solved. Susanne Langer, for example, does not accept the relevance of the biological function of dance prior

to reaching the status of art (*Feeling and Form* (pp. 178–79)).
(Aestheticians do not deal with chronologies, but here this
point is essential.) She dismisses the relevance of the few available examples of "animal dancing" as quoted by Sachs.[54] The
substantial material of dance—human movement—certainly
contains more of the objectively identifiable characteristics
than mentioned in a few sentences by S. Langer (p. 175). She
has had to rely on the only typology of dance that is published
(by Sachs), and she is very much aware that this typology,
because of its shortcomings, is not fully relevant (pp. 191–93).
Following Sachs and other authors, she considers the conquest
of gravity as the main attribute of dance as an art (p. 194). But
there are dance types in existence which, on the contrary, are
directed into the ground, stressing the weight (for example,
many of the "primitive" peoples' dances). There are also many
dances of ecstatic character which keep the dance parallel to
the ground in a circular movement (for example, circling religious dances); and what about the Polynesian sitting dances?
It is true that the conquering of gravity is one of the characteristics of dance as an art, but it is not necessarily the only or
the main one. The acceptance of dance art in the form that
it has reached contemporary urbanised people, who have lost
their "mythic consciousness," is erroneous. One has to respect
the simple truth that the child's mentality is not intellectually
orientated, and that it resembles, to some extent, the mentality
of a "primitive." Therefore, the relevance of dance in its primary form, reaching into the remote past of human existence, is
more than justified for the education of contemporary man.

In these attempts to establish generalisations about dance,
one can clearly see that there is a lack of factual support; there
is not as yet a validated body of knowledge concerning dance
fully established, in spite of many attempts to advance this area
of studies, and dance, being an element of human culture, has
first to be investigated with methods specific to its material.
Before that has been done, any philosophic generalisation
must be hampered. Choreology[55] is in the course of being developed, and is still far behind any other area of human studies.
Owing to this it cannot yet give the aesthetician the needed
information, and certainly these generalisations cannot go as
yet beyond the collected evidence in a particular area of
studies.[56]

REFERENCES

1. L. B. Lawler: *The Dance In Ancient Greece*, p. 138.
2. *Ibid.*, p. 135.
3. *Lucian of Samosata from the Greek*, trans. W. Tooke, pp. 231–33.
4. *Ibid.*, pp. 231–32.
5. Plato: *Laws*, trans. R. G. Bury, Book VII, Vol. II, pp. 91–97.
6. J. E. Harrison: *Ancient Art and Ritual*, p. 47.
7. Aristotle: *Poetics and Rhetoric*, Part I, paragraph 2, pp. 5–6.
8. A. Levinson: "The Idea of the Dance from Aristotle to Mallarmé." In: *Theatre Arts Monthly*, Vol. IX, no. 8, New York, August (1927), p. 572.
9. Athenaeus: *Deipnosophistai*, (14, 269B).
10. Cicero: *Speeches, Pro Murena*, (6, 13).
11. St. Augustine (354–430 A.D.) was especially responsible for introducing Platonic ideas to the teaching of the Church, not only in strictly philosophic matters, but also on ethics and religion.
12. C. Dawson: *The Making of Europe*, Chapters 3 and 4.
    L. E. Backman: *Religious Dances in the Christian Church*, pp. 14 *ff.*, 18 *ff.*
13. L. E. Backman, *op. cit.*, p. 13.
14. *E.g.* dancing in the churchyards, disturbing the order of church services, resulting from unsuccessful adaptation of "pagan" rites, etc. (Backman, p. 22).
15. L. E. Backman, *op. cit.*, p. 22.
    Th. P. van Baaren: *Selbst die Götter tanzen*, p. 36 *ff.*
16. J. Huizinga: *The Waning of the Middle Ages*, Chapter 23.
17. *Orchesography*, trans. C. W. Beaumont, p. 19.
18. According to Rameau (*Maître à Danser*, (1725), trans. C. W. Beaumont, pp. 74–75), the King had his daily dance class for some hours with Beauchamps over the span of twenty-two years. Following this example, every aristocrat in this period had his dancing master in residence.
19. J. Gregor: *Kulturgeschichte des Balletts*, p. 215.
20. *Ibid.*, p. 204.
    A. Levinson: "The Idea of the Dance from Aristotle to Mallarmé." In: *Theatre Arts Monthly*, Vol. IX, no. 8, New York, August (1927), p. 575.
21. P. Brinson: *Background to European Ballet.*
22. P. Rameau: *The Dancing Master*, trans. C. W. Beaumont, p. xii.
23. J. G. Noverre: *Letters on Dancing and Ballets*, trans. C. W. Beaumont, p. 9.
24. These letters were included by Noverre in the second volume (*Programme de Grande Ballets Historiques ...*) of his work in the Warsaw version. It is a manuscript of his writings contained in eleven large volumes and presented to the Polish King, Stanislas Poniatowski, in 1766. It is now being kept in the University Library in Warsaw. The letters deal with a project of a ballet script by Noverre to Voltaire's poem "Henriade." There are also two of Voltaire's letters included expressing his high estimation of Noverre's ballet scripts.
25. P. Rameau: *The Dancing Master*, trans. C. W. Beaumont, pp. 81–82.
    G. Taubert: *Rechtschaffener Tantzmeister*, p. 556.
    C. Sachs: *World History of the Dance*, p. 396, (p. 267, German ed.).
    M. Wood: *Advanced Historical Dances*, p. 31.
26. M. Rehnsberg: *Swedish Folk Dances.*
27. L. Witzig: "Nordisches Volkstanztreffen in Helsingfors 7.-10. Juli 1950." In: *Heimatleben*, 24th year, nos. 1–2, (1951).
28. M. Karpeles: *Cecil Sharp. His Life and Work.*
29. A. Helms-Blasche: *Bunte Tänze wie wir sie suchten und fanden.*
30. I. Guest: *A Gallery of Romantic Ballet*; *The Romantic Ballet in Paris*; *The Romantic Ballet in England.*

31. T. Gautier: *Histoire de l'Art Dramatique en France depuis Vingt-cinq Ans* (1858–59), six volumes; *The Romantic Ballet as seen by Théophile Gautier*, trans. C. W. Beaumont.
32. "Classical" meaning here "academic, following rules."
33. P. Valéry: *Degas. Danse. Dessin.* Chapter 2.
34. H. Bergson: *Essai sur les Données Immédiates de la Conscience*; *La Pensée et le Mouvant.*
    D. Priddin: *The Art of the Dance in French Literature*, pp. 137, 141, 151, 164, 166.
35. H. Spencer: *The Principles of Psychology.*
36. J. Locke (1632–1704), English philosopher.
37. F. W. A. Froebel (1782–1852), German educational reformer.
38. After K. T. Preuss, *Ursprung der Religion und Kunst* (very subjective judgments).
39. Curt Sachs' book was translated into English in 1937, and has been republished several times since then. There are, however, omissions in relation to the German original, which may be misleading, especially if one has to refer to explanatory details and documentation. (For example, fifteen and a half pages of references in the original are reduced to six pages in the English version.) The many footnotes have been entirely left out and this sometimes affects the content.
40. R. Laban: *Effort* (in collaboration with F. C. Lawrence); *Mastery of Movement*; *Principles of Dance and Movement Notation*; *Rudolf Laban speaks about Movement and Dance.*
41. Laban tried to propagate dance through the "movement choirs" (Bewegungschöre) that he called into life all over Europe. These amateur dance groups performed dance for the sake of experiencing it. After many trials he concluded his experiences in the book *Modern Educational Dance.*
42. R. Laban: "La Danse dans l'Opéra." In: *Archives Internationales de la Danse*, no. 1, Paris, January (1933), pp. 10–11.
43. R. Laban: *Die Welt des Tänzers*, p. 3.
    "I would like to expect that my presentation will fall on fertile ground and that more authorised people than myself will put it in the right words which will provide a universal base for the dance's images. Also, the train of thoughts must be extended and certainly corrected many times. This is especially valid in scientific, philosophic and other areas which go beyond my professional experience, and which I have presented not as a professional researcher but as a layman according to the best of my knowledge. My aim is not to establish norms and dogmas, but to awaken the understanding of dance."
44. R. Lange: "Every Man a Dancer." In: *Anniversary Issue* (1971), The Laban Art of Movement Studio, Addlestone.
45. T. Shawn: *Every Little Movement.*
46. F. W. Taylor, (1856–1915), American engineer who established scientific industrial management.
47. Laban was born in Bratislava (Slovakia) of Hungarian parents.
48. R. Laban: *Effort* (in collaboration with F. C. Lawrence); *Mastery of Movement*; *Principles of Dance and Movement Notation*; *Rudolf Laban speaks about Movement and Dance.*
49. O. Szentpál: "Versuch einer Formanalyse der ungarischen Volkstänze." In: *Acta Ethnographica Academiae Scientiarum Hungaricae*, Vol. VII, (1958), pp. 3–4.
    G. Martin and E. Pesovár: "A Structural Analysis of the Hungarian Folk Dance." In: *Acta Ethnographica*, Vol. X, nos. 1–2, Budapest, (1961), pp. 1–40.
    E. Pesovár: "Les types de la danse folklorique hongroise." In: *Studia Musicologica Academiae Scientiarum Hungaricae*, Vol. VII, Fasc. 1–4, (1965).
    G. Martin and E. Pesovár: "Determination of Motive Types in Dance Folklore."

In: *Acta Ethnographica, Academiae Scientiarum Hungaricae*, Vol. XII, nos. 3–4, (1963), pp. 295–331.

G. Martin: "Considérations sur l'analyse des relations entre la danse et la musique de danse populaires." In: *Studia Musicologica Academiae Scientiarum Hungaricae*, Vol. VII, Fasc. 1–4, (1965), pp. 315–38.

K. Petermann: "Syllabus der Volkstanzanalyse." In: *Journal IFMC*—Volkstanz-Kommission Arbeitsgruppe Terminologie. Publ: Im Auftrag des National-komitees für Volksmusik der DDR, July (1965).

R. Lange: *Taniec ludowy w pracach Muzeum Etnograficznego w Toruniu*; "Kine-tography Laban (Movement Notation) and the Folk Dance Research in Poland." In: *Lud*, Vol. L, (1966), pp. 378–91.

F. Marolt and M. Šuštar: *Slovenski Ljudski Plesi—Koroške*.

G. Pajtondžiev: *Makedonski Narodni Ora*.

50. A. Lomax: *Folk Song Style and Culture*; "Cantometrics—Choreometrics Pro-jects." In: *IFMC Yearbook* (1972), pp. 142–45.
51. E. Cassirer: *An Essay on Man*.
52. S. K. Langer: *Philosophy in a New Key*; *Feeling and Form*; *Problems of Art*.
53. M. Sheets: *The Phenomenology of Dance*.
54. C. Sachs: *World History of the Dance*, pp. 9–11.
55. Meaning the knowledge on dance. This term has been used recently in a different context by Rudolph Benesh, who misleadingly named his system of dance nota-tion "choreology."
56. S. K. Langer: *Philosophy in a New Key*, p. 179.

Chapter 2

Rhythm and Dance

As we have seen in the previous Chapter, many authors, in trying to describe the essence of dance, stress rhythm as its outstanding factor. But there are many different meanings attached to the term "rhythm" or "rhythmic."[1] This fact has caused much confusion in the area of music and poetry, but even more so in the area of dance, which cannot claim, even contemporarily, the backing of a well-founded discipline (as can music with musicology).

The all-penetrating property of rhythm makes it a very difficult feature to define. The different opinions vary between acknowledging rhythmical freedom or accepting only rhythmical strictness. Also the criterion of "periodicity" is explored by the different authors in very contrasting ways.[2] Popularly, many practitioners of dance still tend to identify rhythm with its form as it is found in *metrically* performed music. This approach is common in the Western world and it has developed over centuries of music practice. It was especially sanctioned by the European music school of the nineteenth century, and the "official" music of that time.

Only in the late nineteenth century, with the discovery of the different types of music of Asia and that of the disregarded European peasants, were some rhythmic "irregularities" admitted to concert music, in the works of such composers as Bartók, Kodály, Stravinsky.

In fact, there are countless possibilities of rhythm contained within "the extremes of chaos and metronomic lifelessness." This acknowledgment of Curt Sachs leads up to a broad perspective of rhythm in modern times as presented so convincingly in his study.[3] The solution that he proposes to the problem of identifying the rhythmic possibilities is the one that we are following up in this book.

The common appearance of rhythm is conditioned primarily by the cycles created by all the main geophysical periods. This is followed by biological rhythms which are deep-seated patterns of activity in all living beings.[4] Indeed, the human body itself functions rhythmically, for example, breathing and the action of the heart.

The concept of rhythm stems from our experience of basic bodily actions connected with the use of weight in space and time. After going "down," one has then to go "up" in order to be able to move further. This has already formed natural sequences of stresses. The symmetrical nature of the body also imposes basically repetitive patterns of movement. One good illustration of this principle can be observed in the manner in which a man walks: "left-right, left-right."

Thus it is not surprising that the basic movement functions have been used to identify the elementary units in rhythm. This is even mirrored in the terminologies used to describe rhythm in different languages, for example Greek "pous" or Latin "pes" for foot, referring to the metrical units in prosody. Rhythm will be found in any human action and obviously is not confined to music. Some authors in fact maintain that rhythm is perceivable in any visual and spatial art, such as sculpture, architecture, painting, etc.[5] Movement is involved in the creation and perception of any form of art, and where there is movement, the time factor is present. The time factor present in all human action is generally used in an organised way, thus observing a rhythmic structure.

Actually, Greek antiquity left us some very clear definitions concerning rhythm. It is only that the further development of Western civilisation led man so far away from the ability to perceive rhythm in its many appearances in nature and in ourselves and use it spontaneously that the ancient definitions have recently had to be "rediscovered."

Plato (428(??)–348(??)) explained rhythm as the "order of movement" (kinéseos taxis).[6] He acknowledged only two types of movement as non-rhythmical:

(1) kinetic chaos (for a modern example, the thundering of an avalanche);
(2) kinetic continuum (for a modern example, smoothly gliding objects, cars, planes, sailing boats, the flow of liquid from a tap).

Aristoxenus of Tarentum[7] (about 370 B.C.), a pupil of

Aristotle, called rhythm the "order of times" (taxis chronon). Curt Sachs points out that Andreas Heusler added the following sentence to the Aristoxenian definition: "Gliederung der Zeit in sinnlich fassbare Teile" (organisation of time in a way capable of being identified by the organs of perception).[8]

We do understand that all physical happenings, including human movement, occur in space and time, and that rhythm, according to the above-quoted formulations, orders all time-bound events into periods of some regularity. In this way, it would be difficult to imagine any human movement occurring without rhythmic organisation. *Rhythm is an integral part of movement.* Therefore it seems to us that the frequently applied description "rhythmical dances" is a wrongly used application of the words "rhythm" and "rhythmic"—if we agree to follow the meaning as used in the way explained above. One should perhaps say instead "rhythmically or metrically stressed dances," or "dances with strongly developed rhythm," etc.

Starting our survey with the least strict organisation of time, we have to mention *free rhythm*. This is not to be identified with chaos. It belongs to earlier stages of biological development, and is shared by animals. In this kind of rhythm recurrent elements may not occur, but a phrase is discernable, shaping the movement sentence.

It is also a well-known fact that children do not easily follow strictly measured time units. It is only at the age of about nine that the child, in its development, completes the comprehension of time, co-ordinated movements and speeds.[9] Strictly measured time units were introduced by man only in later stages as a symptom of extreme organisation.[10]

Some authors follow free rhythm by *organic rhythm*. This is connected with the action of self-expression,[11] and very often forms irregular periods which are not necessarily strictly metrical. However, within all these irregularities one is able to distinguish specified formations. This may be seen at its best in dances of many primitive peoples and European peasants where dance still remains an art commonly applied and generally known, and often contains an element of improvisation. This touch of freedom makes the "metre" non-metrical to different degrees. In fact it makes it more human.[12]

The *metrical rhythm*, if strictly followed in measured time units, actually restricts the spontaneous expressiveness of the human body. It may best be experienced in the performance of the metronome itself, and it is well known how difficult it is to follow these mechanically measured time units.

This brings us to the *metronomical or mechanical rhythm.* The rhythmic patterns of machines of all kinds are entirely alien to living beings, because they exclude the element of recuperation in movement, as each effort must be balanced organically with an element of recovery.

Rhythm has the property of organising the flow of movement in different ways (*see* Fig. 1). Here we have in mind the progression of accents and stresses making movement articulated. Because of this, rhythm is the driving and shaping force in movement. A rhythmic pattern may be established by the units of a certain length of time that recur in movement. This is the principle of organising the *metrical rhythm.* But a rhythmic pattern may equally be established by use of stresses. This is the *accentual rhythm.*

These two above-quoted possibilities are not separate. Indeed, they combine with each other in many different ways.

Additionally we have to point out that the accentual rhythm may be a result of applying stresses of a specific amount of energy or intensity. This is the *dynamic accent.* The other possible way of creating stresses is by modifying the rate of movement, the tempo. This is the *agogic*[13] *accent.*

Tempo is indeed a very important element of interpretation. We are able to define as a "normal tempo" one which refers to man's way of walking at a leisurely pace. It is clear that the "normal tempo" will vary slightly from one person to another. We can speak in this instance about a "personal tempo." But there are also physical limits to the amount in which one can accelerate or retard the pace of a walk.

There is also the psychological tempo, referring to our mood in interpreting movement. It may have a driving quality or it may have a hesitating expression.

We know also how varied may be the interpretations of "slow" or "fast" tempo as presented by different people, (for example, the different time taken by conductors in performing the same piece of music).

It is also well-known that even a strictly metrical piece of music when performed will induce some slight deviations in timing in order to allow the introduction of some expressive element, to make it indeed human.

This is even more relevant with "primitive" and peasant peoples who are still not bound by the type of imposed and

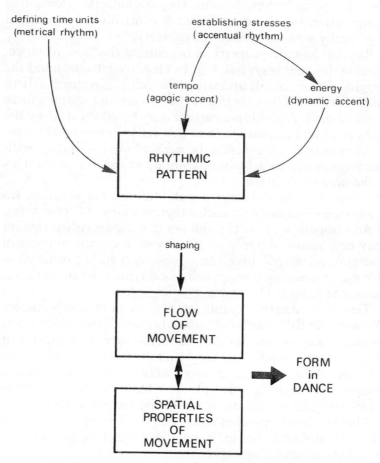

Fig. 1 The organising property of rhythm.

measured strictness as attained by "civilisation" (urbanisation, Westernisation). In their conditions of life there is not yet a striving for mechanical discipline. There is still the possibility of manifesting and acknowledging the primary potential of human movement as revealed directly through the body. The many extensions of our capacities, among the specialisations and appliances of the urbanised world, are simply not *needed* yet. This fact has caused many misunderstandings which have led to a total disregard for the "underdeveloped" or "primitive" people, or to pitying them for not having included in their inventory the latest technological achievements of the Western world.

Their "irregular" music, often following entirely different harmonic criteria, has in addition been labelled by "knowledgeable" musicians as "non-harmonic" and the people themselves "non-musical." For example, the nineteenth-century editions of folk-songs are full of these "mercifully" corrected tunes, made accessible to the "civilised" world for performance on the drawing-room piano.

Even though one may have a sympathetic attitude, the wrong means are often selected in trying to bring help to these people, as not enough is commonly known about their patterns of culture or about their real needs.

We and they are simply on different and incomparable levels, and one should not attempt to apply criteria that are valid somewhere else.

With these people, the arrangement of rhythmic patterns follows a non-rational interpretation. They rely on intuition rather than on control.

The differing emotional stresses are very relevant here and it would be difficult or even impossible to apply any of the criteria to which one is accustomed in Western civilisation. As Curt Sachs concludes in his book:

> "All over the primitive world, accents and meters, their strength and their nature, are conditioned by factors sometimes beyond our insight and reasoning powers."[14]

The rhythmic pattern in this primarily "free," interpretation has a pulsating character closely following the bodily processes of tension and relaxation.[15]

A very good example of one of these manifestations can be experienced in the manner of interpretation described as *tempo rubato*. This musical term applies to elasticity and flexibility within the tempo and rhythm, which is different from rallentando, ritardando, accelerando, or the dramatic pause, and is

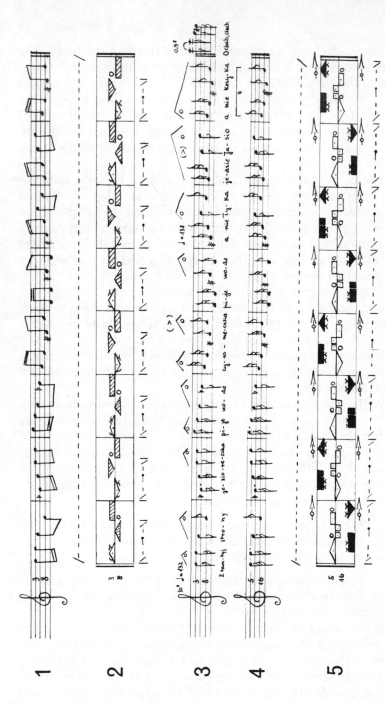

Fig. 2 A synoptic table from fieldwork material.

executed in a specific manner. One takes a minute part of time from one unit and adds it either to the preceding or the following one, causing the structure to fall out of balance repeatedly, although one brings the phrase back to the beat at the end. It is a situation of "give and take within a limited unit of the time-scheme."[16] Every "stretching out" is compensated by a "drawing in" and vice-versa, with a consequent return to the beat ("in good time"). (There is also a return to the beat in the case of rallentando or accelerando, but it is to a beat which occurs sooner or later than it would normally have done; we are not back where we were, for time has been permanently lost or gained.)[17]

This method of dealing with rhythm and tempo is not evidence of bad time-keeping—as some of the nineteenth-century amateur folklorists tried to interpret it, because it did not fit in with their rigid system of music notation. It is, in fact, evidence of an incredible musicality on the part of the performer. It is based on improvisation. The "game" lasts over a relatively short time-span owing to the fact that human attention is limited, especially in the case of "primitive" people.[18] The same may be said about peasants from old rural areas of Europe.

The enclosed synoptic table (*see* Fig. 2) illustrates the problem on hand by one selected example. It is the result of my field-research carried out between 1954–60 in the old rural area of Cuiavia (Poland). (45 villages and settlements were investigated.)[19]

The first line contains the music example as interpreted by a town musician and notated in the metrical manner.

In the second line the dance is notated as it has been performed by the townspeople and landed gentry. Again it is metrical. The choreotechnic units are equally measured, and there is a limited and strictly regular amplitude in moving the body whilst transferring the weight.

Line three contains the same music example, but this time as performed by a genuine village musician who has no idea of music notes and who has never been schooled in music. It is played in the way in which it has "always" been played. The musician has to follow the dancer, the song having previously been improvised by the dancer and taken over by the musician. There is a constant interaction between these two. The

⌒o⟍ signs above the stave indicate the movements when the "rubato" takes place.

Line four is a musicological reinterpretation of line three. In the course of the "rubato" the time units inside the bars remain the same as in lines one and three. The inner structure, however, has been rhythmically remodelled. One could even approximately transcribe the village version to a $_1{}^5_6$ beat instead of $\frac{3}{8}$.[20]

Line five contains the choreotechnic scheme of the same dance as interpreted by the villagers. Indeed, it is only manageable in conjunction with the music of line three, as a five beat with different stresses caused by the hesitant type of stride. The amplitude of movements occurring with the transference of weight is incomparably greater than in version one. There is an inner vibration in the upper part of the body resulting from the intricate change of weight in the feet. The whole performance is entirely immersed in the flow of dancing.

When improvising the song prior to dancing, the performer would indicate the rhythmic patterns with bodily movements, more or less on the spot, which followed the scheme shown in the enclosed table. But the arms and the upper part of the body of the dancer would move in counter-directions, and would follow an entirely different rhythmic pattern,[21] making the whole movement picture even more complex.

Here we come across a polyrhythm in the dancer's body. This is also evident in many of the "primitive" peoples' dances.[22] Furthermore, to fill in the rhythmic phrase, which is longer than the song itself, the dancer adds a series of meaningless syllables at the end of the song (line three).

I think it becomes evident from this example that similar individual solutions enable countless variations of rhythmic patterns to be built up even in the same geographic area. In spite of the great variety of solutions they all represent a defined *type of interpretation* which contributes to the outcome of a particular local style. This also shows that man, in contrast to animals, is able to produce his rhythms and impose them on his body. This is where man goes beyond his own biology, and of this capacity Plato was well aware.[23]

Rhythm is the shaping factor in dance, but it is not yet the form itself. In the case of dance one has additionally to take into consideration the spatial properties of movement employed. They may have their own expressive contribution to offer, but they follow simultaneously the rhythmic pattern of the dance, as the patterned flow serves as a warp to the final weaving of the form in dance.

As a primary factor, rhythm is not only familiar to each living being individually, but it is easily identified by a group and used in its activities as an organising factor.[24]

The universality of man's response to rhythm explains the ease with which it can be transmitted. Living beings are affected by particular rhythms, which are therefore of great importance for intercommunication from the earliest stages of life onwards.

In spite of the constantly growing remoteness to the effect of these properties in the course of civilisation, they may still be found to a varying extent in all human groups, and even in contemporary European civilisation.

The war drums of "primitive" people, and its more modern equivalent, the chanting of slogans at mass meetings and rallies all provide examples of this inherent property. We also know how quickly rhythmically stressed dances such as "rock and roll" spread all over the world, in a manner which one author has compared to the rapid spreading of an infectious disease.[25]

Man has always used rhythm as a co-ordinating factor in his group activities, whether in dance or in working actions. Examples from all over the world can be given of groups executing their work to the accompaniment of songs, sometimes containing the rhythms of the work itself, or to a beat of drums, clappers, etc. Karl Bücher, in his famous book on *Work and Rhythm* explains this convincingly. For an individual performance of a given task, one may follow a rhythmic pattern maintained in one's mind. There is not necessarily a need to expose this pattern externally. But in order to unify a group of people performing a common task, the rhythmic pattern of the action has to be revealed so that everybody can act in the same way. This is even more necessary if the technological equipment is poor and most of the work has to be done only by human hands.

A rhythmic pattern thus imposed and applied to the physical task to be performed, has a psychological effect on the workers.

The maintenance of the working action, with the exclusion of non-essential elements, brings, by its uniformity and continuity, a relief and ease to the performers. There is no need to establish every action anew or to rethink the structuring of the physical action every time according to the particular result aimed at. Thus the mental effort is diminished. This degree of automation is, on that level, still beneficial to the executor of the task, but then the rhythm is not yet being dictated by a machine. The song or drum beat applies a suitable rhythm, constructed according to the psychophysical capacity of the human being. The effort is in this way always well-balanced by the element of rest and recovery which follows the element of activity and strain.

The type of rhythmic pattern, as well as the words or slogans used in songs, serve also as an emotional stimulus. They spur the performer on to activity and they take his attention away from the physical exertion of the task itself.

To this extent we can follow Bücher, as his argument is logically well-founded in his book, and is supported by a vast collection of documentary and experimental proof. But he goes too far in generalising the effect of working rhythms on human beings. This all derives from his tendency to make "work" nearly "sacred" and an all-pervasive factor of human activities (*see* Chapter 1).

The way in which movements can become automatic within such a rhythmic framework causes a sense of relief and is experienced as a stimulating happening, lifting the worker above the drudgery of toil. It may indeed inculcate an element of elation and excitement, so mobilising him to activity and saving waste of energy. It rouses the human being from the everyday monotony and fatiguing heaviness of being conscious only of performing work.

In this way, organised work may resemble dance to some extent, as Bücher points out on several occasions, but he once again goes too far in identifying this type of work performance with dance itself. He clearly does not see that there is a difference in function between a working action and a dance action, resulting from the fact that different movement qualities have to be applied to execute each of them.

In the working action, the aim is physical and objective and the action is organised to accomplish it. There is a concrete physical resistance to be overcome which is proportional to the task to be achieved.

In the dancing action, however, the "doing" is the aim in itself. There is no other objective than to maintain the performance, as the aim is not material. This corresponds with Sachs' definition (*see* Chapter 1) that dance is movement having no utilitarian aspect.

Neither can one accept Bücher's viewpoint that dance rhythms have only developed from working rhythms. If this were so, it would seem a contradiction to us, because before man started to develop his more complex actions—especially those connected with the use of tools—he already knew many other actions employing rhythm, particularly those connected with self-expression and communication. This can already be seen in the animal world[26] and is connected basically with the "dance-like" actions of display which have nothing to do with the performing of physical tasks. A baby, before it is born, moves in the womb and performs rhythmic patterns which have some communicative and expressive significance, such as discomfort or pleasure.[27]

As rhythm is an integral part of movement, we shall have now to turn to the latter in considering further facts necessary in our investigation.

REFERENCES

1. Compare: *The Oxford Companion to Music*, (1970), p. 872; *The Oxford Dictionary of English Etymology*, (1967), p. 765; *Fowler's Modern English Usage*, (1966), p. 526; *The Concise Oxford Dictionary*, (1969), p. 1071; *Encyclopaedia Britannica*, (1971), Vol. XIX, p. 288.
2. E.g. *The Oxford Dictionary of English Etymology*, (1967), p. 765, explains rhythm as "metrical movement or flow as determined by the recurrence of features of the same kind." *Encyclopaedia Britannica*, (1971), Vol. XIX, p. 288, defines rhythm generally as an "ordered alternation of contrasting elements." Further on, it includes a note that there are wider conceptions of rhythm that "include in it even non-recurrent configurations of movement as in prose or plainsong."
3. C. Sachs: *Rhythm and Tempo*.
4. F. A. Brown, Jr.: *Biological Clocks*.
   J. L. Cloudsey-Thompson: *Rhythmic Activity in Animal Physiology and Behaviour*.
5. In about 330 B.C. Aristoxenus of Tarentum had stated this.
   M. Wahl: *Le Mouvement dans la Peinture*.
   E. Souriau: *La Correspondance des Arts*, p. 77.
   The Nature and Art of Motion, ed. by G. Kepes, especially the article by S. W. Hayter.

R. Bayer: "The Essence of Rhythm." In: *Reflections on Art*, pp. 186–201, (from *Revue d'Esthétique*, Vol. VI, no. 4, (1953), pp. 369–385).

6. Plato: *The Laws* 665.
7. Three books of his still survive, containing his *Elements of Harmony and Elements of Rhythm*.
8. A. Heusler: "Deutsche Versgeschichte." In: *Grundriss der Germanischen Philologie*, Vol. VIII, Berlin, (1925), p. 17.
9. J. Piaget and B. Inhelder: *The Child's Conception of Space*, p. 418. *See also* pp. 61, 65–66, 416, 467.

    J. Piaget: *The Child's Conception of Movement and Speed*, Chapter 10, "Conservation of Uniform Speeds and their Relationships."

    J. Piaget: *The Child's Conception of Time*.
10. C. Sachs: *Rhythm and Tempo*, pp. 21, 65–67.

    C. M. Bowra: *Primitive Song*, p. 85.
11. "Self-expression" meaning "expression of oneself," but already containing some creative element, even if in a rudimentary state. This is evident with children.
12. C. Sachs: *Rhythm and Tempo*, p. 12.
13. H. Riemann: *Musikalische Dynamik und Agogik*.
14. C. Sachs: *Rhythm and Tempo*, p. 48.
15. *Ibid.*, p. 45.
16. *Oxford Companion to Music*, p. 894.
17. *Ibid.*, p. 894.
18. C. Sachs: *Rhythm and Tempo*, p. 35.

    C. M. Bowra: *Primitive Song*, pp. 34–35.
19. R. Lange: "Kinetography Laban (Movement Notation) and the Folk Dance Research in Poland." In: *Lud L*, (1966), pp. 378–91.

    R. Lange: "Tańce kujawskie." In: *Literatura Ludowa*, no. 4, (1964), pp. 13–20.
20. This is the proposed analysis reached by ethnomusicologists, directed by the late Prof. M. Sobieski in Warsaw. (Published in the magazine *Muzyka*, (1960), no. 3, p. 40.)
21. Compare Sachs, *Rhythm and Tempo*, p. 37.
22. A. Lomax: *Folk Song Style and Culture*, p. 237 *ff.*

    A. C. Fletcher: *Love Songs among the Omaha Indians*, part on rhythm.

    C. Sachs: *Rhythm and Tempo*, p. 40: "Such counter-rhythms are in the primitive world exclusively instrumental—a proof that, technically, they stem from muscular impulses."
23. Plato: *Laws*, I, 654B.

    See also: T. Georgiades: *Musik und Rhythmus bei den Griechen*, p. 37.
24. Bücher gives impressive evidence of this.
25. J. A. M. Meerloo: *Dance Craze and Sacred Dance*, p. 35.
26. C. Darwin: *The Expression of the Emotions in Man and Animals*.

    H. Ellis: *Studies in the Psychology of Sex*, Vol. 1, part II, pp. 35–41.
27. J. A. M. Meerloo: *Dance Craze and Sacred Dance*, p. 13.

    J. A. M. Meerloo: "Archaic Behaviour and the Communicative Act." In: *Psychiatric Quarterly*, Vol. XXIX, (1955), pp. 60–73.

Chapter 3

Movement—the Material of Dance

Since movement is the essential material of dance, it is amazing how little this basic element has been explored in most of the published works on dance. It is much as if the analysis of sound material were missing from musicological investigations.

In order, however, to identify all observable manifestations of human movement, a very complex system of analysis and notation has been needed, and its lack has hampered the outcome of rational choreology. It is here that we turn to the theory of movement brought forward by Rudolf Laban,[1] for it was only after he had made this system available that adequate works in dance research started to appear, so greatly advancing this area of studies.[2]

After many attempts made over the centuries, it has become possible for the first time to put observations of human movement into the form of a rational statement, as well as to make a permanent record of the results in graphic scripts. In this way each and every movement could be comparatively analysed, so providing the basis for a scientific approach to movement and dance research.

The movements of the human body, as they operate in space and time, are subject to the ordinary laws of physics, and can be objectively observed. Accordingly, in his movement analysis, Laban first establishes spatial models embracing all possibilities of human movement. The criteria he uses follow the old arrangements of contrasts, for example, up–down (described by Laban as "high–deep"), forward–backward ("long–short"), right–left ("wide–narrow"), responding to the three-dimensional aspect of movement. These basic spatial features have double cross-sectional combinations along the diameters of the planes, and triple combinations along the diagonal directions. The ideal geometrical body encompassing all these possibilities is the sphere. Laban concludes this part of his analysis within the arrangements of the icosahedron, which is already close to the sphere, except that the icosahedron (Fig. 3) allows a survey of the orientational points and of the spatial relationships (dynamic tensions) arising between movements going into different directions. This exposes the dynamic interplay as it is continually traceable in movement.

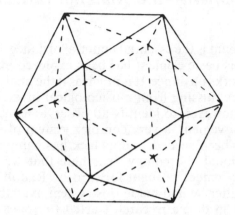

Fig. 3 The icosahedron.

Additional factors controlling these explorations are those of time (for example, slow–quick), and the force of gravity (for example, the higher from the base the movement is made, the "lighter" it becomes; the lower it is made, the "heavier" it becomes). So a practical exploration of the spatial model will make the dynamic changes, being arranged in the ideal way, evident to the mover.

By analysing the properties of human movement within maximum exploration inside the space model, Laban established several movement scales. They result from the functional progression of movement possibilities when passing subsequently through different areas around the mover. They have been called "scales" because of the fact that they show traces of regularity. The basic criteria are again the three-dimensional aspect of movement, explored in contrasting sets, together with the natural capacities of the human body, so conditioning the outcome of certain spatial structures.

The scales are a universal means of reference, enabling us to identify any of the movement examples that we may come across in the incredible wealth of movement shapes produced by man.

It can easily be deduced from this short introductory survey how these *means* established by Laban could well aid the different areas of human studies where the observation and analysis of human movement is relevant.

By following up this analysis of movement logically, Laban established a system of notation called *Kinetography* (or *Labanotation* in America).[3] This enables us to record the three-dimensional aspect of movement precisely, its extension into any direction, its timing and its continuity. In this way, any movement structure and its dynamics may be analysed and written down.

It is specifically this ability to record movement in its *continuity* which makes Kinetography Laban so much more advantageous than many of the other systems of movement notation.[4] The latter very often only register *static* poses, so leaving one to guess at the connecting movements intervening between them. From the previous Chapter, we may remember the important part that the *flow* of movement (the general progression or flux), has in shaping the form.

If we compare the first two examples in Fig. 4, it becomes evident that the time element affects the shaping of these movements.

In (*a*), the right arm performs a long movement over the first four units of time, and a short one over the next unit.

In (*b*), a short movement occurs over the first unit, and a long one over the last four units.

These two examples are not only rhythmically in direct contrast to each other, they also vary dynamically, as the time and space factors are differently combined. In (*a*) the first movement requires less strength than the one which follows; in (*b*), it is the opposite. A different approach is required to execute each of these movements, and as a result both indicate something different in their expression. In (*a*) after a long introduction there is a short conclusion. In (*b*) after a short introduction there is a long conclusion. In this way, it can be seen how both movement examples are differently formed and incorporate different meanings.

In (*c*) and (*d*) two similar examples confront each other. This time, the movements are started with the arms lowered. The rhythmic patterns are the same as in (*a*) and (*b*), and so also is the shaping, but again the resulting form is different, because a different spatial texture has been applied.

Here we can clearly see that the spatial texture of movement, *together with* the rhythmic pattern, produces the form. The differences are easily perceivable in the four examples in Fig. 4 set out comparatively side by side.

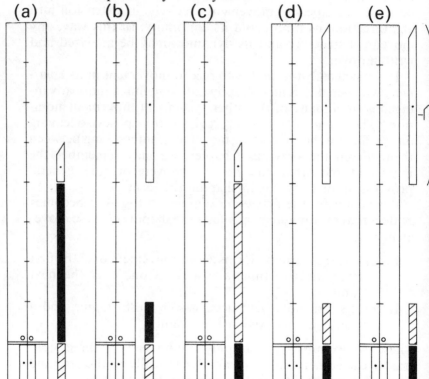

Fig. 4 The shaping properties of space and time.

But man is a complex psychophysical entity, and his inner life also participates in his movement actions. His inner attitudes reveal themselves in his movements, thus giving them some particular characteristics. These may be conditioned by a practical aim, and they express the personal traits of an individual. Additionally, man not only has the ability to rule his rhythms, but he is also able to use different movement textures for the sheer purpose of creating abstract expressions.[5] This trait is beyond the capability of animals and it is in this instance that man again parts company from animals.

The inner life manifestations as observable in movement are the most substantial part of any movement action. This is what Laban technically calls "effort." In order to perform a definite task, a specific "effort" is needed. Success will be obtained if the effort is adequate for the given action. The ergonomics of movement are the decisive criterion here. But it is only possible to execute movements properly if one's "effort" capacity is balanced, and this is connected with the accumulation of inner experience of a person.

Laban, in his "effort" analysis and its notation,[6] enables us to define the "going with" and "going against" attitudes towards motion factors (weight, space, time, flow, in the context of the general flux of movement) in proportional arrangements. Naturally, it would not be possible to convey them by giving absolute dimensions and measurements. But here there is the possibility of recording these manifestations as visible in movement in a *relatively* objective way. This type of solution as given by Laban is something totally new. It was not previously possible to define the manifestations of man's inner life in a dynamic synthesis of movement performance. The ability to define the "effort" in movement terms is essential in order to describe specific ways of movement interpretation.

We may add to our previous sequence the sign of "pressing," (part (*e*) of Fig. 4). This indicates that the second movement is performed with a pressure. This feature is an expressive addition, as it does not result from the dynamic context of movement in our example, nor from any physical task introduced.

"Effort" is even more relevant when it comes to defining those movement forms which are not outwardly exposed. This is particularly evident with babies and infants.[7] The subtle traces of actions observable in the body (technically called "shadow-movements") are essential in revealing personal traits and intentions.[8]

Inner attitudes, as revealed through "effort," show themselves in movement so clearly that they can be "read." They are common and therefore are genuinely comprehensible in the world of living beings.

Their impact may even be sensed in inanimate material which has been treated by man's movement action (for example sculpture, painting). They are also relevant as movement colourings establishing a particular style of dancing.

It is thus convincing that the content of movement, namely that which arises from the inner attitudes, is the basic element of expression and communication; and this may be traced back to the very early stages of man's development, to his biology.[9]

REFERENCES

1. R. Laban: *Effort* (in collaboration with F. C. Lawrence); *Principles of Dance and Movement Notation*; *Rudolf Laban speaks about Movement and Dance*.
2. O. Szentpál: "Versuch einer Formanalyse der ungarischen Volkstänze." In: *Acta Ethnographica Academiae Scientiarum Hungaricae*, Vol. VII, (1958), pp. 3–4.
   G. Martin and E. Pesovár: "A Structural Analysis of the Hungarian Folk Dance." In: *Acta Ethnographica*, Vol. X, nos. 1–2, Budapest, (1961), pp. 1–40.
   E. Pesovár: "Les Types de la Danse Folklorique Hongroise." In: *Studia Musicologica Academiae Scientiarum Hungaricae*, Vol. VII, Fasc. 1–4, (1965).
   G. Martin and E. Pesovár: "Determination of Motive Types in Dance Folklore." In: *Acta Ethnographica Academiae Scientiarum Hungaricae*, Vol. XII, nos. 3–4, (1963), pp. 295–331.
   G. Martin: "Considérations sur l'Analyse des Relations entre la Danse et la Musique de Danse Populaires." In: *Studia Musicologica Academiae Scientiarum Hungaricae*, Vol. VII, Fasc. 1–4, (1965), pp. 335–38.
   K. Petermann: "Syllabus der Volkstanzanalyse." In: *Journal IFMC*—Volkstanz-Kommission Arbeitsgruppe Terminologie. Publ. Im Auftrag des Nationalkomitees für Volksmusik der DDR, July (1965).
   R. Lange: *Taniec Ludowy w Pracach Muzeum Etnograficznego w Toruniu*; "Kinetography Laban (Movement Notation) and the Folk Dance Research in Poland." In: *Lud L*, (1966), pp. 378–91.
   F. Marolt and M. Šuštar: *Slovenski Ljudski Plesi—Koroške*.
   G. Pajtondžiev: *Makedonski Narodni Ora*.
3. R. Laban: *Principles of Dance and Movement Notation*.
   A. Knust: *Handbook of Kinetography Laban*.
   V. Preston-Dunlop: *Practical Kinetography Laban*.
   A. Hutchinson: *Labanotation*.
4. Thus it is not surprising that at an International Congress organised by the German Academy of Science in Dresden, 1957, from among the many systems of notation which were presented, Kinetography Laban was estimated as the one which most fully met the demands of a scientific approach to dance research. D. Stockmann: "Der Dresdener Kongress für Tanzschrift und Volkstanzforschung." In: *Deutsches Jahrbuch für Volkskunde*, Vol. IV, (1958), p. 160.
5. C. M. Bowra: *Primitive Song*, pp. 261 *ff*.
6. R. Laban: *Effort* (in collaboration with F. C. Lawrence).
7. M. North: *Personality Assessment through Movement*.
8. W. Lamb: *Posture and Gesture*.
   W. Lamb and D. Turner: *Management Behaviour*.
   P. Ramsden: *Top Team Planning*.
9. G. Steiner: "The Language Animal." In: *Encounter*, August (1969).
   E. T. Hall: *The Silent Language*, pp. 61–66.

Chapter 4

When Movement Becomes Dance

During a seminar in 1944, Franz Boas introduced an excellent paper and discussion on dance. Very soon, the basic question arose: "What is the relationship of ordinary movement in everyday activity to the movements of the dance?"[1]

In trying to investigate this problem we have to go to the beginnings of dance, finding it in rudimentary forms in the biology of all living beings. Just as nobody would be satisfied in modern times with a course on the history of art which began with the Renaissance, so we have to leave the written histories on dance and commence our survey by turning to the animals.

In spite of many differences, there are still fundamental connections between the world of Man and the world of animals. This is particularly evident in the primeval area of movement, since it is a factor of life in a very basic sense.

Man, in the same way as animals, utilises movement in "everyday actions" in response to the basic necessities of life. This is understandable, for after all, it is owing to his body's animal function and structure that man is considered as one of the primates.[2]

Immediately it can be argued that man's physical actions differ from those of other animal species because of their high standard of specialisation. Nevertheless, sufficient evidence may be produced to arouse serious doubts as to their exclusively human origin, for many of these activities have already been initiated in the animal world.

There is, for example, evidence that not only mammals, but also certain sorts of birds and insects occasionally use "tools" (in the initial state), to extend the instrumental capacities of their bodies.[3] For instance, a bird from the Galápagos Islands, *Camarhynchus Pallidus*, takes larvae from tree holes by means of small twigs, as its own beak is too short. Then there are the American wasps, *Ammophila Urnaria*, which use small stones to pound the sand in front of holes which they have dug. Certain insects even perform typical forms of rearing, such as the ants which keep their "cows," *i.e.* aphides, in order to use the sweet substance which they excrete.[4] The social traits and social organisation of man's life also have their equivalents among animals, again not only among primates but also among insects.[5]

Perhaps many of the older stories concerning animals quoted in literature must be dismissed as anthropomorphisms and classed along with the fables, but this cannot be done with all of them. In the last decades, more material has been collected showing how little is really known about animal life, and especially about the behaviour of animals in their natural setting. Modern works on ethology have not only advanced the knowledge about the mechanisms ruling animal behaviour, but have also drawn our attention to the fact that many of man's behavioural actions are understandable only when related to those observable in animals.[6]

Movement as a means of expression and communication is known equally to animals and to Man. It seems that the more rudimentary any movement expression, the more commonly it is understood by living beings. This is how we "understand" animals and how they understand us.[7]

The primary expressions, however, are confined to biological functions and they, particularly, prove to be contagious,[8] (for instance coughing, laughing, crying, yawning, itching, scratching, shivering, rocking).[9]

Some of these primary communicative and expressive actions include dance-like movements which are known among all living beings. According to some psychologists they already commence in foetal life. When floating in the amniotic fluid, the child performs active movements of rotation, flexion and stretching during the second half of pregnancy.[10] This is considered to be spontaneous behaviour, as distinct from the reactive and protective movements executed earlier. Psychologists also consider that the rocking movements mothers use in putting their babies to sleep evoke memories of the prenatal safety; this may sometimes be manifest in the case of schizophrenics when they execute rocking movements.

Human beings sometimes also feel the need to return to the early stages of their own development, to experience once more

Plate 25 (*above left*): "Fishing dance," Kamayura tribe in Xingu, Brazil.
Photo: R. Hanbury-Tenison
Plate 26 (*below left*): an Indian dance representing different birds, Brazil.
Plate 27 (*above*): Aborigines in Corroboree dress, in front of the totem pole, Northern Australia.
Photo: Australian News and Information Bureau

Plate 28 (*above*): Aboriginal Corroboree, Australia.
Photo: Australian Information Service

Plate 29 (*below*): a group of nomadic Aborigines in a Corroboree, Australia.
Photo: Australian News and Information Bureau

Plate 30 (*left*): Aborigines dancing in a Corroboree, Australia.
Photo: Australian News and Information Bureau

Plate 31 (*below*): the "Moon Legend Dance" performed by Aborigines, Bathurst Island, Darwin, Australia.
Photo: M. Brown, Australian News and Information Bureau

Plate 32 (*above*): Aboriginal dancers performing in a Corroboree, Bagot Aboriginal Reserve, near Darwin, Northern Australia, June, 1969.
Photo: Australian News and Information Bureau
Plate 33 (*right*): the story of a kangaroo hunt in a Corroboree, Aranda tribe, central Australia.
Photo: Australian News and Information Bureau

Plate 34 (*above*): the "Brolga," dance of an Australian bird, December, 1969.
Photo: Australian Information Service

Plate 35 (*below*): a tribal dancer attends school regularly to teach traditional skills to the Aboriginal children, Bamyili, Northern Australia.
Photo: M. Jensen, Australian Information Service

Plate 36 (*left*): a group of Mevlevi, Whirling Dervishes, with their orchestra. Picture taken in the courtyard of the Memlevi-Khane Mosque, their former headquarters at Konia, Turkey.

Plate 37 (*above*): dancers sway to the rhythm of a classical dance in hypnotic trance, Ceylon.

Photo: R. J. Chinwalla

Plate 38 (*above*): a demon dancing, Ceylon.
Photo: R. J. Chinwalla
Plate 39 (*right*): a masked dancer in a fertility dance.
Photo: McGeorge

Plate 40 (*above*): dancers with masks, Ceylon.
Plate 41 (*right*): Ram Gopal with his partner, Shevanti, in a classical dance, India.
Photo: G. Nanja Nath

Plate 42 (*above*): the "Ketchak," monkey dance, Bali, Indonesia.
Plate 43 (*left*): dance in Bali, Indonesia.
Photo: H. Bristol

Plate 44 (*above*): the "Tjalon arrang," a dance conveying the triumph of good over evil, Bali, Indonesia. The priests' soldiers, armed with kris, advance on the witch.
Plate 45 (*below*): dance in Bali, Indonesia.

Plate 46 (*left*): the teaching of the Balinese art of dancing.
Plate 47 (*below*): the young dancer portrays a legendary bird, Bali, Indonesia.

Plate 48 (*right*): classical dance, Cambodia.
Photo: Pardon/Dalmas

Plate 49 (*left*): a relief of a dancing girl from the Theatre of Dionysos, Athens, National Museum.

Plate 50 (*above*): professional
weepers employed at ancient
Egyptian funeral, in the tomb of
Ramose, eighteenth dynasty,
Thebes.
Plate 51 (*right*): an eighteenth-
century Turkish miniature from
the Topkapi Library, Istanbul.
Photo: W. Swaai

Plate 52 (*left*): a pottery figure of a dancer, Yüan dynasty (A.D. 1271–1368), China.

Plate 53 (*left*): European classical dance—Alicia Markova.
Photo: Baron

the security of their earliest childhood and its associations with familiar movements. The use of rocking-chairs and swings may be a relevant example here. The indulgence in dances with a strong element of syncopated rhythm may perhaps also be ascribed to this need.[11]

The "dances" performed by certain animals have already had their communicative aspect explored in some depth. For example, worker bees make dance-like movements to tell other worker bees where honey can be found.[12] Also, of course, different forms of "courtship dances" are an important element in the mating of many animal species.[13]

During the mating period in animals, their communicative actions are exaggerated through exhibitionism.[14] These traits are not lost in man, although they are more repressed. Even in human dances, already quite remote from these stages, the sexual aspect is in varying degrees still apparent.[15]

Whatever the motivation, the animal "dances" trace out abstract shapes and fixed floor patterns (circle, line),[16] and it can be said that these "dances" of animals already consist of "stylised" movement actions. Evidently, there would seem to be an elementary appreciation of shape, colour and sound in the animal world, which could not have been initiated by man.[17] For this reason, in trying to distinguish between the dance activities of man and animals, it is no longer acceptable to support the contention that there is a lack of shape in animal "dances."[18]

On the other hand, it seems that it would be difficult to draw an absolute line indicating where "dance" does start on this level. Many of the spontaneous movement actions acquire some dance-like appearance quite imperceptibly, the transition from everyday-life movement to "dance" is blurred.

In conjunction with this problem, the seemingly superfluous and useless repetitive movements performed by children and young animals, often labelled as merely "playful," must be mentioned. There have actually been many attempts to define the aspect of play in human and animal life.[19] Herbert Spencer, for example (*Principles of Psychology*), explains play as arising from the necessity of young living beings to get rid of surplus energy (here, he follows the ideas of Friedrich von Schiller).

Much more insight, however, is given by Charles Darwin in his attempt to explain this problem.[20] According to him, the reason for the urge of living beings to perform dance-like actions is the need to relieve emotional tensions—by means of movement—caused by joyful as well as by disturbing events. This has often been reported in descriptions of "primitive" peoples,[21] but children and animals react in the same way. Everyone has experienced, for example, the sight of a child hopping when embarrassed, or a dog running round in circles when overwhelmed with joy.

Similarly, the need to relieve the feeling of discomfort resulting from excessive use of particular joints in specialised, restricted everyday movements like sitting hunched over an office desk or before a conveyor belt in a factory, may provoke spontaneous, dance-like actions, thus providing a natural counterbalance.[22]

For all these reasons, the value of play for the development of a child has been recognised and included in the educational process. I would like to introduce here an interesting interpretation given by Laban.[23] According to him, the play actions of children and animals are simply an unconscious practising of "effort" actions (which means more than just the practice of skills as indicated by Groos); a way in which young creatures try out different types of movement qualities necessary for the mastering of different actions when they are fully grown and will have to face in real life situations.

But these are all examples of dance still playing a *physiological* role in the life of human beings as well as that of animals, and are directly connected with biological functions.

This may remind us of the *recapitulation theory* brought alive by the works of Charles Darwin and applied to psychology by the American scholar, Granville Stanley Hall.[24] It follows that the ontogenetic stages observable in the development of a single child mirror the historical development of man (phylogeny). This idea in its primitive form has long been discredited, as there are no direct, identical counterparts traceable. But one cannot *entirely* dismiss the existence of some parallels and reminiscent manifestations observable in a single man's development, and comparable to *some extent* with stages of human development in general, including that of animals.[25]

And there are some parallels evident between the child and "primitive" man.[26] The fact that in both cases there are limitations in the areas of their experience does not entirely explain the existing similarities. The child and the "primitive" are still in total agreement with the biological background. This may be the reason why it is so difficult for the already alienated, urbanised, and adult person to penetrate alike the world of the child and the world of the "primitive."

It may not be without relevance that Professor Jean Piaget produced his integrated system of developmental psychology and revealed so clearly the growth of intelligence,[27] because of his previous biological studies. Man, although he creates his culture, does not cease to be a biological being. Man, being the unique species, has to act in his own special way, but at the same time according to the laws of his biological make-up. As soon as this is brought out of balance, disturbed human beings are the result. This is especially evident in man's technological development; in the course of gaining mechanical substitutes, man is often confined to inactivity which excludes the "formative or creative mental processes," the positive element in any productive action.[28]

It therefore becomes evident that knowledge of the biological aspect of dance not only has significance as yet another element in the historical perspective of human development, but indeed, it has great contemporary value that has still not been explored and appreciated enough. The biological aspect of dance has educational (especially as regards infants and younger children), recreational and rehabilitative relevance.

These "dance" manifestations still continue to be executed spontaneously by children even in our technologically-oriented age. They may not belong to art, they may not be included in investigations led by aestheticians, but nevertheless they are an essential part of human development. Fighting or ignoring them will result only in the production of more unbalanced human beings.

In rehabilitative or recreational work these primeval dance faculties may be employed to a different degree, even in conjunction with more specified dance forms and traditional ways of moving. The activation of the living being may be re-introduced in this way, thus restoring to it what has been lost on the way to an advanced technology.

We are not trying to pursue here any specific form of "evolutionism" or any other "isms." We have simply to respect facts which undeniably have a profound relevance to human life.

At this point, a quotation of Sir Herbert Read might perhaps be relevant:

> "Unless we can discover a method of basing education on these primary biological processes, not only shall we fail to create a society united in love; we shall continue to sink deeper into insanity, mass neuroses and war."[29]

For explanations involving other aspects of dance, we must turn first of all to that which is connected with the spiritual development of man, that which has caused him to grow away from the animal world. In spite of the fact that animals possess the ability to learn to a limited degree,[30] and show signs of intelligence, they certainly lack the ability to think in abstract terms, and to direct their actions. Additionally, they do not possess language, script or creative imagination,[31] which are the unique attributes of man's spiritual development.

REFERENCES

1. F. Boas: *The Function of Dance in Human Society*, pp. 17–18.
2. W. La Barre: *The Ghost Dance; the Origins of Religion*, p. 517.
3. E. A. Armstrong: *Bird Display and Behaviour*.
   W. Goetsch: *Vergleichende Biologie*, pp. 90–92.
   Sire: *L'Intelligence des Animaux*.
4. J. T. Moggridge: *Harvesting Ants and Trap-Door Spiders*.
   W. Goetsch: *op. cit.*, pp. 115–16, 135.
   F. Schwangart: "Tierpsychologie." In: *Forschungen und Fortschritte*, Vol. XX, (1944), pp. 85–93, (includes bibliography of publications dealing with "tools" and "rearing" in the animal world).
5. M. R. A. Chance: *The Nature and Special Features of the Instinctive Social Bond of Primates*.
   U. C. Wynne-Edwards: *Animal Dispersion in Relation to Social Behaviour*.
   K. Lorenz: *Studies in Animal and Human Behaviour*.
   K. Lorenz: *On Aggression*.
6. K. Lorenz: *Studies in Human and Animal Behaviour*. However, there is a strong criticism of this contention, *see:* A. Montagu: *Man and Aggression*.
7. C. Darwin: *The Expression of the Emotions in Man and Animals*.
8. J. A. M. Meerloo: "Archaic Behaviour and the Communicative Act." In: *Psychiatric Quarterly*, Vol. XXIX, (1955), pp. 60–73.
   K. Lorenz: *Studies in Human and Animal Behaviour*, p. 220.
9. For example, the action of someone coughing in a church or concert hall will usually be repeated by several members of the congregation or audience, etc.
10. J. A. M. Meerloo: "Archaic Behaviour and the Communicative Act;" *Dance Craze and Sacred Dance*.
    M. Minkowski: "Neurobiologische Studien am Menschlichen Fötus." In: *Handbuch Biologischer Arbeitsmethoden*, Vol. V, (1928).
    L. Carmichael: "Behaviour During Fetal Life." In: *Encyclopaedia of Psychology*, New York, (1951).
11. J. A. M. Meerloo: *Dance Craze and Sacred Dance*.

12. K. von Frisch: *The Dance Language and Orientation of Bees.*
13. Quoted by C. Sachs: *World History of Dance*, pp. 9–11.
    M. von Boehn: *Der Tanz*, pp. 7–8.
    K. Groos: *Die Spiele der Tiere; Die Spiele der Menschen*, pp. 350–51.
    H. Ellis: *Studies in the Psychology of Sex*, Vol. I, Part 2, pp. 29–41.
14. J. A. M. Meerloo: *Communication and Conversation.*
    K. Lorenz: *Studies in Human and Animal Behaviour*, p. 190.
    H. Ellis: *Studies in the Psychology of Sex*, Vol. I, Part 2, p. 51.
15. H. Ellis: *Studies in the Psychology of Sex*, Vol. I, Part 2, pp. 41–58.
16. C. Sachs: *World History of Dance*, p. 11.
    Also, for example: C. Appun: *Unter den Tropen*, p. 468.
    J. Maclaren: *My Crowded Solitude*, p. 66.
    K. Groos: *Die Spiele der Menschen*, p. 113.
17. Film by Heinz Sielmann: *The Secret Bowers*, shown on BBC 2 (British television),
    27th October, 1968 — pre-nuptial rituals of the Bower and other birds showing
    traces of aesthetic sense.
18. Brought forward by F. Böhme, "Massstäbe zu einer Geschichte der Tanzkunst,"
    In: *Geist und Gesellschaft. Kurt Breysig zum 60. Geburtstag*, Vol. II, Breslau, (1927).
19. H. Spencer: *The Principles of Psychology.*
    K. Groos: *Die Spiele der Tiere*, (1896); *Die Spiele der Menschen*, (1899).
    J. Huizinga: *Homo Ludens*, (1938).
    S. Millar: *The Psychology of Play*, (1968).
20. C. Darwin: *The Expression of the Emotions in Man and Animals*, (1872).
21. *E.g.* R. Thurnwald: *Psychologie des primitiven Menschen*, p. 171.
22. K. Groos: *Die Spiele der Menschen*, pp. 471–73.
    H. Steinthal: *Zur Bibel und Religionsphilosophie*, p. 248.
23. *Mastery of Movement*, pp. 16–17.
24. *Adolescence*, (1904).
25. K. Lorenz: *Studies in Human and Animal Behaviour*, pp. 134, 150, 186, 187, 190,
    220, 229, 252, 254–56, 272–73, 276, 278, 290, 297, 300, 312, 323, 327, 352–53, 358,
    364, 370 (all entries on human behaviour).
    F. M. Cornford: *From Religion to Philosophy; A Study in the Origins of Western
    Speculations.*
    H. Kelsen: *Society and Nature.*
    E. von Topitsch: *Ursprung und Ende der Metaphysik.*
    A. I. Hallowell: "Self, Society and Culture in Phylogenetic Perspective." In: *Evolution after Darwin*, ed. Sol Tax, Vol. II, (1960) pp. 359–62.
    B. Rensch: "The Laws of Evolution." In: *Evolution after Darwin*, Vol. I, (1960),
    p. 103.
    S. Tax and C. Callender: *Evolution after Darwin. The University of Chicago Centennial*, (1960), Vol. III, *Issues in Evolution.* Discussion in Panel 2: "The Evolution
    of Life." On p. 124 the formulation of processes of development given by Sir Julian
    Huxley.
26. E. von Topitsch: "Phylogenetische und Emotionelle Grundlagen Menschlicher
    Weltauffassung." In: *Filosofia, Saggi Filosofici*, 9, Torino, (1962). (Reproduced in:
    Kulturanthropologie, ed. Mühlman and Müller, (1966).)
27. J. Piaget: *The Origin of Intelligence in the Child.*
28. H. Read: *The Origin of Form in Art*, p. 149.
    R. Fox: "The Cultural Animal." In: *Encounter*, July (1970), pp. 31–42.
    G. Steiner: *Language and Silence*, Part I.
29. H. Read: "The Biological Significance of Art." In: *Saturday Evening Post*, Philadelphia, 26th September, 1959.
30. J. Dembowski: *Psychologie der Affen.*
31. F. Kainz: *Die "Sprache" der Tiere.*

Chapter 5

Dance Becomes Art

Dance, common in the animal world as a biological means of expression and communication, takes on a new function with the ascent of human beings—that of expressing abstract ideas. This is because man is the only one among all animals capable of conceptual thought.[1] Movement, being the most primordial means of communication, was the medium through which man primarily revealed his ideas. Thus movement becomes a means of *human* expression which cannot be interchanged with verbal description. Movement conveys sophisticated meanings in a more compact and rapid manner than speech. In this way, it is closer to the biological existence of man than language with its code system already verbally externalised.[2]

This specific "movement thinking" was man's first step in self-expression on his way to spiritual life and creativity. This element is inherent in dance, and was presumably the forerunner of thinking by word-symbols.[3]

There is no doubt that language is the highest achievement of man in creating *his* world, thus consequently escaping the direct pressures of nature, but non-linguistic codes have been known in the living world before man evolved, and they continue to infiltrate into language, giving it specific colourings and meanings.[4] Without them, even contemporary language is deprived of one of the most expressive elements of its composite whole. Live speech has the additional enrichment of expression owing to the accompanying bodily actions.

One could perhaps even say that without bodily movement, language would not primarily have been possible. Phrasing and articulation are movement-conditioned, conveying, in their variability, the intentions of the speaker. Only in further stages, when language reaches superstructures of logical thought (for example, tenses, metaphor), does it move away from the primeval base of human expression.

This may be the reason why the most "primitive" peoples, who have a limited vocabulary and language system, at the same time have rich content in their dances.

In the art of dancing the spiritual experience of man is revealed directly through his body, this being the only instrument essential to dance. The dancer externalises concepts created in his mind through his physical body. This double role of the dancer as the creator and as the instrument externalising the creation is unique in art. The involvement of man in spiritual capacities (using imagination, creativity in dance) gives him a chance to reach human heights whilst at the same time using his animal body to the full extent, not suppressing its needs, but relieving, balancing them in the most coherent way.

Some time ago it was pointed out that the physiological results of dancing are identical with the physiological results of pleasure. Dance provides both narcotic and stimulating effects at the same time. In this way, it gives happiness and relief to the man involved.[5]

The human body produces natural symbols through its physiology. Being expounded in dance they become more and more abstract. This is even more so if social distance is being introduced. The physiological processes are then correspondingly hidden.[6]

Dance as an art is directly concerned with the spiritual life of man, and belongs primarily to his spiritual culture. This is perhaps the basic criterion by which we can distinguish between "dances" executed by animals and man's art of dancing. Man must have achieved this specialisation very early on, as dance forms are present in prehistoric rock and cave paintings, and as they are evident among "primitive" people. C. Sachs states that since the Stone Age no new forms or contents have been incorporated into the art of dance, furthermore, that the creative process of dance was already concluded in prehistory.[7]

This statement brings our attention to the high standard of art achieved by prehistoric and "primitive" man in general. The content is most sophisticated, but is transmitted directly. The form is very functional and economic. This balance between form and content has never been surpassed in later stages of human development, and never again has man so genuinely and directly expressed himself in art. It seems to prove that "artistic and mental development does not have to proceed parallel with advancement in material civilisation."[8]

Nowhere is this more relevant than in dance. Already early in human history dance had achieved the status of art and perhaps also that of the first art of man. In the course of further development this compactness and uniqueness of dance as an art became successively replaced by other specialised areas of expression—sound, music, speech, poetry, drama.[9] There is good reason to consider dance as the initial art. Even if it cannot be proved historically, it seems convincing if the progressive development of the human faculties are taken into consideration. Indeed, man has gradually become more and more remote from dance. There is no need, for instance, in our civilisation to restrict oneself only to one's body to express creative ideas. There are so many areas in art which have gradually eliminated the *direct* participation of man in the act of art itself. It is a generally acknowledged trait in urbanised civilisation for people to participate passively in art—the object of art becoming more and more externalised. Alien material such as stone (sculpture) and sound (music) has replaced the human body. Dance has become only one of many means of social entertainment, and a traded art.

In spite of becoming art, dance is still made up of the commonly used human movements. However, it becomes transformed from everyday movement, with its practical, utilitarian objectives, into the poetry level of bodily actions in space.[10] Here the irrational and spiritual element takes over. The aim is to reveal content arising from the mind's creativity. This content is understandable as a purely expressive entity; it cannot be explained by other media than dance.

Laban gives a detailed technological explanation of the difference between dance and everyday movements. According to this theory of movement, the basic movement elements (space, weight, time, flow) are employed in dance actions as well as in work actions. They are simply stressed differently in each of them. This is because different functions are required for movement in work actions and dance actions. As a result, the observable quality of movement in dance is quite different from that in everyday actions.

In work, the element of *weight* is the most stressed first of all. While performing a physical task, the weight to be moved, lifted, etc. has to be overcome by application of a specific amount of energy. In dance, the most important element, and that which is stressed first, is the *flow* of movement. The extent to which it is applied in dance has no practical equivalent in everyday actions.[11]

The remaining elements of movement (time, space and weight) in dance are of secondary importance, and they may be stressed in different ways. For example, the element of time is very clearly exposed in rhythmically stressed dances. The element of space may be of significance when spatial structures prevail in a dance. The weight factor may additionally be stressed when the dance has a bouncing character.

The "flow of movement," being so primarily stressed in dance, determines at the same time the substance of dance. Movement action in dance has no practical function, it is only through its continuity, its "lasting," that the phenomenon of dance is evoked. Without respecting the continuity, without stressing the element of "flow" in movement, there is no dancing action; the "flow" of movement is the warp of dance. Therefore a dance exists only as long as the dancer is actually dancing. This does not mean that he has to travel constantly—even when holding a pose the dancer is able to maintain the attitude of continuity—but if this is dropped, he will immediately be eliminated from the context of the dance.

From this, it becomes clear that the dance action is not connected with utilitarian aims. Using human movement in this transformed setting, dance acquires a different function in man's life. As an art, dance becomes abstract not only in its function, but also in its texture.

The criterion distinguishing the non-utilitarian aspect of movement as characteristic of dance has been brought forward by C. Sachs. It seems to be a very well-founded argument.

In the light of the above explanations, it becomes evident why people are able to dance even after hard work. Many ethnographical observations give us accounts of peasants returning from a full day's work in the fields and then enjoying a whole evening of dancing, even continuing well into the night. It seems that on these occasions the dance actions serve as a direct counterbalance to the work actions, not only psychologically, but also physically, because of the different ways in which the movement in work and in dance is structured.

The same explanation applies to the feats of "primitive" warriors, who, on returning from long and exhausting marches, are still capable of producing astonishing energy in executing dances. Very often these dances go on through several nights with only very short breaks for sleep.[12]

It is remarkable how often in ethnographical fieldwork one comes across old people or people weak and ill who become lively and much refreshed when they start to produce their old dances. It is quite understandable, of course, that such a return to the "good old days" must be very stimulating emotionally. But, at the same time, one notices that the action of dancing must itself have some special physical characteristics which are different from everyday actions, and which enable old people to execute what are sometimes very demanding movements. In addition to this it is clear that there must be a very strong spiritual background behind the physical manifestations of such dances. This is well illustrated by the following example.

in the old rural area of Northern Poland it has long been the custom to dance for the good growth of crops and flax. Everybody dutifully performs the dance on Shrove Tuesday in order to counteract any possible disaster during the year. In this particular instance, even an old woman from the village of Kożyczkowo,[13], who was seriously ill, dragged herself out of bed so that she also could join the ritual.

From my own fieldwork I would like to quote another interesting example. An old peasant man had been ill for several years and unable to do any hard work, but on several evenings he danced in the village and was not over-exhausted. The villagers were very angry with him, thinking that if he could dance he should also be able to work. This man explained to me confidentially that dancing did not demand of him the same "strength" as that of work.

As is general in art, the activity of dancing is connected with the joy of self-expression, and results in satisfaction achieved from creative activity. It is here that the aesthetic urges of man come alive. Again, this has not been initiated by man; some of the biologically-founded animal activities (for example, courting behaviour) reveal an appreciation of shape, colour, and sound. One can trace some rudimentary elements which could be acknowledged as being in a remote way akin to "art," as, for example, adornments, song and dance.[14] It seems that aesthetic needs, however highly developed by man, are deeply rooted in his biological past.

For the "primitive" man, dance has great importance in his life.[15] The adornment and dress for dance activities are prepared with the utmost care. For example, the painting of the body, and the use of flowers for decoration are intended to stress the attractiveness of the body, but at the same time there is an aesthetic estimation of the adornments themselves.[16]

This is even more true of the execution of dances; the manifestation of life experience expressed through these created forms and symbols provides aesthetic satisfaction. All this combines to create a positive stimulus, binding people to life and providing them with the necessary courage to face life in their hard conditions.

Laban's interpretation is that the aesthetic pleasure in dance is derived mainly from the feeling of balanced "effort capacity" achieved through involvement in dance activity. After the disturbances and frustrations of everyday life, man feels the urge to find a different world allowing him to recover his balance; and he turns to art which he creates out of his imagination. In "primitive" stages, this is still mainly dance, and the urge to become immersed in it stems from his "deep-rooted need to keep alive the effort balance."[17] It is only this state of balanced effort capacity that enables man to face life anew, to accomplish new tasks and to perform necessary actions in the most appropriate and effective way.

REFERENCES

1. H. C. Elliott: *The Shape of Intelligence; the Evolution of the Human Brain.*
   G. W. Hewes: "Primate Communication and the Gestural Origin of Language." In: *Current Anthropology*, Vol. XIV, nos. 1–2, February–April (1973), pp. 5–24.
2. G. Steiner: "The Language Animal." In: *Encounter*, August (1969), p. 7.
3. W. Wundt: *Völkerpsychologie. Eine Untersuchung der Entwicklungsgesetze von Sprache Mythus und Sitte*, Vol. III, "Die Kunst," (1919 ed.) p. 5.
   W. La Barre: *The Human Animal*, p. 58.
   C. M. Bowra: *Primitive Song*, p. 261.
4. G. Steiner: "The Language Animal." In: *Encounter*, August (1969).
5. H. Ellis: *Studies in the Psychology of Sex*, Vol. I, Part 2, pp. 53–57.
   K. Groos: *Die Spiele der Menschen*, p. 112.

60   The Nature of Dance

6. M. Douglas: *Natural Symbols; Explorations in Cosmology*, pp. 12 *ff*; *Purity and Danger*.
7. C. Sachs: *World History of Dance*, pp. 6, 62.
8. A. Lommel: *Prehistoric and Primitive Man*, p. 15.
9. C. M. Bowra; *op. cit.*, pp. 261–63.
10. Diderot claimed in his time that dance is poetry (*see* Chapter 1). H. von Schurtz: *Urgeschichte der Kultur*, p. 498.
11. R. Laban: *Modern Educational Dance*, pp. 95, 96, 102, 103.
12. P. Wirz: *Dämonen und Wilde in Neuguinea*, p. 124.
13. After B. Stelmachowska: *Rok obrzędowy na Pomorzu*, p. 101.
14. C. Sachs: *World History of Dance*, pp. 9–11.
    V. Junk: *Handbuch des Tanzes*, pp. 240–41.
    E. Grosse: *Die Anfänge der Kunst. See also* Chapter 4.
15. G. Buschan: *Neue Beiträge zur Menschen- und Völkerkunde*.
16. B. Malinowski: *The Sexual Life of Savages in North Western Melanesia*, p. 298.
17. R. Laban: *Mastery of Movement*, p. 140.

Chapter 6

Dance—the Vehicle for Spiritual Activities

In talking about the beginnings of dance, one cannot avoid turning to the beginnings of art in general. Many different explanations have been put forward concerning the ascent of art.[1] However, there is a tendency to agree that all surviving painted and sculptural representations executed by prehistoric man, as well as the art of the still existing "primitive" peoples, were a response mainly to a necessity to *use* something powerful rather than to look at something nice, as Professor Gombrich explains it.[2] This is because the problem of survival of early and primitive man demanded more than only the development of skills for securing food and defence. His practical knowledge was indeed considerable,[3] but as a thinking being man also had to explain the facts surrounding himself. As soon as these went beyond the capacities of his experience, mythical explanations were introduced.

These explanations were based on the belief that actions and words technically unrelated to a phenomenon can exert upon it a physical effect. All magical practices logically follow this principle.[4] Indeed, the principle of association is the basic trait in the working of the human mind, and is employed equally in magic and in science. The difference is, however, that in science (also in the science of "primitive" man), man relies on experience gained in his direct fight for survival and is supported by observation. In magic, man relies on emotional experience observed in himself and is conditioned by his hopes and desires.

For these reasons, Malinowski indicates that some similarities exist between magic and science, calling magic a pseudo-science.[5]

As man, in his primitive conditions, was exposed to the mercy of nature, he created magic from his ideas, thus providing himself, according to his belief, with a powerful, practical means which allowed him actively to influence the course of nature. In this way, man believed he was able to improve and to safeguard his existence as well as to fight his enemies. Thus in magic the three basic needs: productive, protective and destructive, were followed.[6]

There is good reason why "primitive" man did not reject the magician's tricks, even if they were obvious to him or if some doubts were cast over his mind. In his conservative approach he strictly followed the well-established patterns which had proved "effective" over generations; turning to them he found a feeling of security in the familiar ways of life.[7]

People resort to magic when human knowledge and skill fail.[8] This is not remote from the behaviour of any human beings; under the appropriate conditions people will often feel and react in a similar way.[9] For instance, in times of war and cataclysms, if no other support is available, an otherwise intelligent and educated person is suddenly found to be capable of accepting the help of para-rational means (such as talismans, etc.). It fulfills the psychological need for reassurance. Even if magic did nothing more to prehistoric and primitive man than give psychological support in organising the human group and strengthening its social bonds, it had a constructive aspect in these circumstances.[10]

Professor Gombrich gives helpful guidelines on the function of art in the life of "primitive" and prehistoric man.[11] With the aid of a few examples, he creates a helpful perspective leading to the understanding of the significance of magic in art in the past and revealing connections with contemporary civilised human beings.

In spite of differences in cultural background there seems to be a "fundamental sameness of mental processes" amongst all mankind. If man's mental equipment has ever differed from the existing general norm it must have been a long time ago, when man first began to distinguish himself from animals, for "no trace of a lower mental organization is found in any of the extant races of man."[12]

Because of its biologically-rooted universal appearance among human beings, dance became an art early on. As F. Boas says, dance is an outlet for accumulated emotions in motor activities, and it takes on specified forms.[13] In this way, it may express thoughts and transmit ideas.[14] The content may be very sophisticated, but it is instantly communicated to the receiver. It is not describable by words and is understood intuitively. With its direct influence on performer and onlookers, dance gained a magical and mystical significance. Thus dance was predestined from the beginning to serve as a medium for magic and religion. This trait is commonly found in all cultures.

At the same time, the form that evolves in dance, as in art in general, casts an "aesthetic spell" on the receiver. "The form and its meaning combine together to elevate the mind above the indifferent emotional state of every-day life."[15] This experience is also one of the factors that contributed to the strengthening of "primitive" man's beliefs in the power of magic.[16]

In order to set a historical framework for our further investigation into the application of dance in the different types of culture, a few facts from prehistory in relation to Europe must be mentioned here.

The food-gatherer and hunter cultures evolved in the remote past, and the application of dance in hunting magic, is evident both in the Paleolithic cave paintings and among the still existing "primitive" peoples who pursue this type of economy.

Even amongst the oldest existing cave and rock paintings representations of dance are found.[17] For example, the paintings of sorcerers, as in the cave Les Trois-Frères (Franco-Cantabrian area) from the late Paleolithic age, show people dressed up in animal masks and involved in some sort of dances which presumably are connected with hunting magic.[18] Similar representations exist in the cave paintings of Altamira (Northern Spain) and in the fine engravings of Teyjat (Dordogne).[19]

Also from the late Paleolithic age there survives a painting in Cogul (Catalonia)[20] showing a circle dance, consisting of nine women surrounding a man. This presumably represents a fertility rite in conjunction with hunting magic. In actual fact, it is not clear whether the figure of the man in the centre of the circle has been added at a later period. It is not unusual to find that later ritual-performing peoples have superimposed new paintings on to the old, regardless of the appearance of the resulting whole,[21] a sign that these magic practices have a recurring validity.

In one of the caves at the foothills of the Pyrenees (Grotte du Tuc d'Audoubert in Ariège) heelmarks were found in front of a clay hillock. These have been interpreted as the foot imprints of a group performing ritual dances.[22]

The dressing up in animal skins was not just a fancy masquerade. The early hunter still felt himself to be in unity with nature as he took part in the life of his environment.[23] Animals were still considered equal beings, and man was made to feel transformed into the animal if he put its skin around himself.[24] This mode of thought may have given rise to totemism.[25] The need to kill the animal must have caused deep conflicts in the mind of early man and a whole magic complex was evolved to counterbalance the effects of this disturbing event. The animal, gaining a spiritual aspect in hunter cultures, gave rise to the idea of the ancestral animal and the belief in the animal's soul. This was, according to some scholars, extended to all objects, (animism[26] and animatism[27]). Together with this belief in spirits and souls, ancestor worship must have come into existence.

Sometime around 3,000 B.C. peoples inhabiting the areas of Eastern Europe and Western Asia began to develop cattle herding. A nomadic type of life was the result and in effect the pastoral cultures evolved, causing the attitude of man towards the animal to change profoundly.

Under the influence of the mature Middle Eastern cultures (10,000–4,000 B.C.) new types of cultures emerged in Europe *c.* 2,000 B.C. The primitive farming techniques successively imposed themselves upon the older cultures of foodgatherers and hunters and led finally to agriculture.

These changes again caused an entirely different relationship between man and the environment. He became preoccupied with the fertility of the soil. A new outlook on life was gradually established,, and with it new symbols were employed.

This is mirrored in the cave paintings which survive in Eastern Spain, (called, a little misleadingly, the "Second Hunter Style"). Here, human figures can be seen in motion either independently or combined with hunting scenes or other activities. A different style of dancing is also to be found in these

Neolithic paintings in the caves of Minateda, Jimena de Jean-Cueva de la Graja, Tivisa-Font Vilella, Cueva de Los Letraros, Cantos de la Visera.[28] The tradition of rock painting was not only known among the prehistoric hunters and foodgatherers in south-western France and northern Spain, but also, in different periods, in North Africa, southern Africa, Scandinavia, Siberia, the Americas, Australia, and the Far East. Not only did this tradition appear over vast areas and in different periods, but sometimes it also continues to be lived out in our own era by certain "primitive" peoples.[29]

This provides the vital link that enables the meaning of the images in cave and rock paintings of prehistoric times to be identified—at least with some certainty. Similarly, the archaeological pictures representing dance scenes may be supplemented by studying the dance cultures of contemporarily existing "primitive" peoples. They often live in conditions similar to those of the prehistoric foodgatherers and hunters, and even if we admit the possibility of changes and outside influences, the prevailing form of dance among them is still impressive enough to give us an idea of the function of dance in human life at that stage,[30] as for example the Veddas in Ceylon,[31] Semangs in Malaya,[32] Bambuti Pygmies of the Ituri forest in the Congo,[33] Bushman tribes in South Africa,[34] Papua tribes from New Guinea,[35] the Australian Aborigines,[36] the Yahgan and Alacalufs Indians from Tierra del Fuego,[37] and the Californian Indians.[38]

The necessity to contact the spirits, to appease them or to influence their will is regarded by some scholars as the beginning of religion as distinct from magic, the latter dealing with straightforward actions in reaching the desired practical aim, for example, the higher one jumps the higher the flax will grow. According to Frazer, for example, religion is "a propitiation or conciliation of powers superior to man which are believed to direct and control the course of nature and of human life."[39] But one has to point out that some magic dealings are concerned with spirits too, and in many religious rites the magic element is present. It is difficult to know where the dividing line is.[40] For this reason, some authors prefer to define them together as a "magico-religious" complex.[41] Frazer also thinks it probable that magic arose before primitive religion in human history;[42] but there seems to be no evidence on which to base this assumption. At many levels of culture, they existed together.[43] Mircea Eliade states clearly that it is impossible to reach the origins of religion because no primary evidence is in existence;[44] all viewpoints on this matter must rely on speculation or belief.

Also, evolutionary growth did not proceed everywhere in the same manner. Not all peoples passed through the same stages of development, nor was progress constantly evident on the way. On the contrary, stages of degeneration and regression may have been involved.

Trance and ecstasy are often employed in connection with magical practices. Trance may be induced spontaneously or by means of hypnosis. In this state, only a dim awareness of what is going on prevails, and the participant may reach a deep state of trance, catalepsy.[45]

These dissociational states of mind become ritualised and are given a formal shape in connection with religious practices. They will be interpreted in different ways in different cultures, and they may be associated with many different institutions and practices. Their distribution is very wide and their origin presumably very ancient.[46]

Different techniques are used in order to bring about the state of trance. Sometimes it is done by the use of drugs,[47] or by the infliction of long-lasting fasting periods, very often in conjunction with different rites, etc., leading to exhaustion and hallucinations,[48] but one of the main means employed all over the world at various times has been dance.[49]

Dance as a means of achieving trance has a physiological effect on the brain of the performer and thus promotes dissociation. (Hyperventilation, exhausting, whirling, turning, circular, rotational movements—all affect the sense of balance and equilibrium, and eventually cause dizziness.)[50] It must have been early on that "primitive" man discovered the trance-like property of dance if performed in particular circumstances. This was associated with a primarily pleasant experience leading to autohypnosis and ecstasy. In this way, the participants were liberated from the day-to-day experiences of mind and body.[51]

Sometimes in certain magical dances, as a result of self-hypnosis, the dancer identifies himself completely with the animals he is representing. For example in Java, the hypnotised dancer eats very coarse grass without harming himself in any way.[52] In achieving the paranatural state of mind, the dancer really believes that he is a snake, kangaroo, bird or even a plant.[53] It is not surprising that this new "reality" was accepted as an experience on a different level, connected with meeting spirits, beings of the "other" world, etc. With the decline of his will-power, man is ruled by the moods and ideas induced by his beliefs.[54]

According to E. Bourguignon, dance is here used in three decisive instances: to initiate dissociation (to "invite" the spirit), to portray the characteristic motion of the spirit, and to help in dispatching the spirits.[55] The execution of dance, often leading to exhaustion and unconsciousness, is used as a method of exorcising—removing the "alien spirit"—and for healing.

The state of visionary trance and ecstasy are the attributes of Shamanism.[56] The shaman lets his soul go on "a journey," visiting places and meeting spirits.[57] There is evidence that shamans from all over the world use dance in this context, as for instance in Siberia, Tibet, Mongolia, China, Malaya, North and South America and Australia.[58]

A different type of trance is connected with possession. The emphasis here is on the impersonation of spirits; it is always a group phenomenon, and is intimately related to dance.[59]

Possession trance combined with dance is evident (after E. Bourguignon) particularly in West Africa;[60] among the descendants of Africans in the Americas, Cuba, Jamaica, Haiti ("voodoo" cult), Trinidad and Brazil;[61] Indonesia, Bali;[62] Java;[63] South-east Asia, Malaya, Vietnam, Thailand and Cambodia.[64]

In rites or forms of worship connected with religious beliefs, prayer is always present, and sacrifice is essential. Offerings are made on different crucial occasions and the act of worship becomes formalised in ritual.[65] Similarly, in some instances, possession trance becomes highly ritualised. Dance is employed to a large degree in ritual, intensifying the effect on the participants.

Dramatic material was incorporated into the content of ritualistic dances to transmit to the worshippers the stories of gods, demons and heroes—the accumulating mythology. Together with the motifs of victory of life over death and with honouring the dead, these were, in all probability, the factors which contributed to the outcome of dance drama performed in temples and shrines.[66]

Dance drama was used primarily to interpret and transmit epic content. Detailed human features were gradually ascribed to the gods, and the performers who represented them originally expressed all the god's characteristics by movement only, dance being the basic element in these rituals.[67]

As the story-plots of dance rituals became more complex, it was no longer possible to convey them only by the medium of dance, and mime and speech had to be included in order to make the narrative content clearer.[68] In this way, the ritualistic dance drama of ancient civilisations came into existence. Its eventual secularisation formed the beginning of theatre.[69]

The religious dance drama of Indonesia and of South-east Asia originates from highly ritualised possession trance. It has also been pointed out that there is a resemblance between the drama produced by the "Burmans, Talaings, Javanese, Siamese and Cambodians; and it would be interesting to investigate their common origin, which appears to be South Indian."[70] Indeed, the dance drama in South India has reached its peak with Bharata Nātyam and Kathākali.[71]

"The words for actor (nata) and play (nataka) are derived from the verb nat, the Pankrit or vernacular form of the Sanskrit nrit 'to dance'."[72] Also the royal theatre in Cambodia is called Rung-ram, "dancing shed."[73] These are additional indications of how the dance has been the origin of drama.

The same applies to the origin of drama in Chinese and Japanese civilisations. The mimetic dances of Ancient China must originally have been connected with ancestral and fertility rituals.[74] This eventually developed into the specific type of Chinese theatre, where dance, mime, acrobatics, song and music are united.[75]

In Japan, the ancient Shinto religious dances (Kagura) were said to have the power to contact the gods and bring relief to the souls of the dead.[76] The Kagura dances originated (according to the oldest historical document of Japan, the Kojiki), when the goddess, Ame no Urume, lured the offended sun goddess, Amaterasu, out of the cave where she was hiding, and causing the whole world to be immersed in darkness.

Kagura gave rise to the Gagaku[77] (court music and dance),

the Noh[78] (the classical theatre), and Kabuki (the popular theatre).[79]

Similarly, in Ancient Greece dance played an important part in the ancestral cult. In early days, the tragic chorus and its dithyramb were closely attached to the rites performed at the tombs or shrines of heroes.[80] The dithyramb was a hymn originally performed in honour of Dionysus, the god of wine, fertility and vegetation.[81] The festival to honour him was performed all over Greece and included processions involving orgiastic elements. The dancing Maenads formed part of the train of Dionysos and contributed, in particular, to the frenzied character of these rituals.[82]

Aristotle pointed out that tragedy originated from improvisations of the leaders of the dithyramb,[83] and that it was only in the fifth century B.C. that Aeschylus (525–456 B.C.) diminished the part played by dance, which was performed by the chorus.[84]

The dramatic element in dance as such is, in fact, always present because there is a dialogue between contrasting elements (*e.g.* the individual—his moods and reflections; two or more people facing each other—structural tensions in a group composition, etc.).[85]

However, dance also continued in its function as a vehicle for spiritual activities in many religions, and sometimes still does so in the present day.

As we have already mentioned, in the early Christian world, dance was one of the ritualistic elements inherited from the Graeco-Roman and Jewish past. The early Christian Church had to follow this tradition of the antique world before developing its own media. As dance was at one time part of any religion, this is not surprising.

Even with the rising tendency in the then young Church to exclude "pagan" elements, the dance survived for some time, for there was clear evidence in the Holy Scriptures that King David had danced before the Ark (II Samuel, 6). In the second century it was declared that angels danced in heaven (Platonic ideas incorporated into the Church's philosophy), and it was therefore very advisable for Christians to include dance in church services. Dances were also performed in the churchyards to honour the early martyrs.

It is highly probable, however, that in many countries local dance rituals of "pagan" origin were assimilated. To the horror of the church Fathers this element gradually seemed to be taking over in the then trouble-ridden Europe. Therefore, from the fourth century onwards the Church tried to remove all dancing from its liturgy, but the battle continued for many centuries, and even then resulted only in partial success. Indeed, there are still traces of dance movements visible in the liturgies of the Roman Catholic and Greek Orthodox Churches, as well as the Coptic Christian Church of Abyssinia. In some places in Spain (for example Sevilla), liturgical dances are performed in association with church festivals, and dances are performed in honour of the Virgin Mary in the Basque provinces.

In the Middle Ages in Europe one particular social problem from the thirteenth century onward involved the outbreaks of dance epidemics. These had religious connotations, and were connected with dancing pilgrimages to several shrines where people were said to find relief from the "dance disease," which showed epileptic features. L. Backman tries to explain their outcome mainly in conjunction with the widespread ergotism (poisoning from diseased grain and bread) that occurred in that period.[86] But in the same book he says that the friends and relatives would often substitute for the diseased person and join the supplicatory peregrinations of the dance procession on his behalf, so that they too were entirely involved in the activities of the "choreomaniacs."

Additionally, the hopping dance procession of the saints was continued in Echternach in Luxembourg up until the first World War in periods when there was no longer any ergotism. Healing and protective ritual—remnants from the Middle Ages—also survive in Charleroi, Belgium (region of the Borinage, a mining area). A priest carries the Host to "L'terre al danse" (the place where legend says the dancing mania manifested itself), and the entire group and priest begin to dance, moving speedily forward across the open space.[87]

It is much more probable that the hypnotic property of dance was responsible for the outbreak of these mass psychoses, the ergotism possibly having been an additional factor in some instances.[88]

But the Middle Ages, with its anxiety-ridden population, need not be our only source of examples. A contemporary discotheque with a crowd of youngsters performing some of the latest dances could, with its atmosphere of total involvement and tension, often be put forward as a good example of mass psychosis induced by dance. However, the motivation is different. There is no longer evidence of there being any direct connection with man's spiritual strivings.

Referring to the old peasant dance culture of Europe, which still exists today as a vast complex, it maintains many of the old features of life, in spite of the eradicating tendencies of Christianity and advancing urbanisation. Many of the functions concerning spiritual activities are still there, clearly traceable, sometimes referring back to very remote times.

Actually, there is a visible connection between the art of the vanished "primitive" cultures and those still existing,[89] and similarly there are some links traceable between "primitive" peoples and the peasants of Central and Eastern Europe, in spite of the many big differences. Many components of culture are preserved among peasants which are usually confined to "primitive" peoples, (*e.g.* the extended family system, couvade, matriarchy, totemism, vendetta, the use of the fire-saw and hoe).[90] The astounding fact that these connections have lasted into contemporary times, despite being close to the urbanised Western world, has only recently become of more interest to Western anthropologists.[91]

The functional characteristics of the dance culture among traditional Central and Eastern European peasants have so many connections with old magical practices that they sound amazingly similar to those practised in a "primitive" community.[92] The "Christian" façade is very thin, and without much difficulty one can trace the attempts of the Church to assimilate the dance ritual into its own practices by superimposing new names and contents.

Good examples of this are the dances of the "nestinari" in the Balkan area,[93] or the fire dances of the Anastenarides (Greek Orthodox sect) performed annually in Northern Greece.[94] The dancers hold icons in their hands, and the ceremony is connected with the killing of a consecrated lamb. It is executed to honour St. Helena. In reality, it is presumably a Christianised Dionysian ritual. Only recently (1972) the Bishop Spyridon denounced it as a diabolical orgy savouring of black magic.[95] These unusual feats are explainable by the fact that people who achieve a state of dance-ecstasy are able to do things normally impossible, as for example, to walk on fire without being hurt. This is known among many different cultures, for instance in the Philippines and with the Dyak tribes in Borneo.[96]

There are also still in existence ecstatic dancing practices in the Mediterranean basin which are connected with healing, *e.g.* tarantism and related patterns in Apulia, Sardinia, Spain and Provence; the zar cult of North East Africa; the stambuli or bori cults of Tunisia, Algeria and Morocco.[97] Not only is the bite of the poisonous spider tarantula healed by the dance that eventually leads to exhaustion, but also emotional and psychosomatic disturbances are similarly dealt with.

There have actually been Christian sects who incorporated ecstatic group dances into parts of their worship, for instance the Shakers, in the United States in the nineteenth century; converts to Christian Churches in the West Indies—receiving the Holy Spirit in the tradition of Methodism; Spiritual Baptists in Trinidad and on the island of St. Vincent, Jamaica, Haiti, (known also as "Shakers"); American Indian Christian Churches of the North-western United States.[98]

There have been several Messianic movements, as for example in the late nineteenth century, the "Ghost Dance Movement" which Incorporated Western Indian Tribes of the United States. In achieving hypnotic states, visions were perceived. The people believed that they came into contact with dead relatives and received messages about the nearing end of the world. This combination of old Indian beliefs and Christian ideas was instrumental in the outburst of the tragic Indian uprising of 1890.[99]

Similarly the "Hallelujah Movement" of the South American Indians uses dance to achieve trance (Brazil, Amazon Basin and the Guianas). The motive of their search is a land without evil, without death.[100]

There are also other religions which use dance ecstasy as an element of their worship. A good example may be provided by the religious Muslim sect of "the Whirling Dervishes," the Mevlevi dervishes of Konya (Anatolia). They have a very wide distribution—from the Atlantic coast of North Africa to Malaysia and Indonesia.[101] The origin of their dance ritual may actually have connections with an Ancient Greek ritual (Konya was the home of the Phrygian Dionysus). Similarly the Hassidim (Jews of Eastern Europe) used ecstatic type of dance in their rituals to heighten the mystical powers of the Divine.[102]

From the above-discussed facts, it becomes evident that there are deep-rooted connections between art (especially dance as the primary art form), magic and religion (*see* Fig. 5).[103] This is owing to the unity they shared at the beginning of human history. As soon as art and religion divided, forming

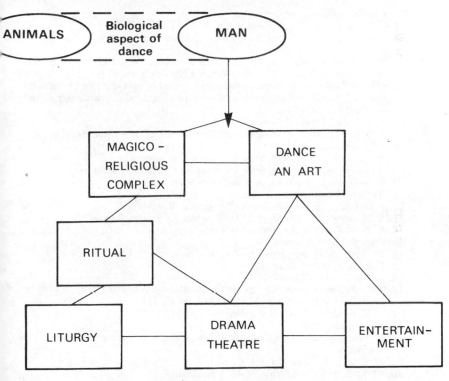

Fig. 5 The lineage of dance.

successively separate specialisations, dance lost its original significance in man's life and was relegated to a form of more or less reputable entertainment or pastime activity. It sometimes even lost its connection with art altogether.

There is a gap between the world of "primitive" peoples and peasant cultures on the one side and the technically developed industrial civilisations of Europe and America on the other.

The latter are no longer mature cultures in the old sense, as they have acquired properties never before known. Since the French Revolution, these new cultures have based their form and order on economic and political, rather than on religious or cultural, motifs.[104]

REFERENCES

1. F. Boas: *Primitive Art*, pp. 13–16.
2. E. H. Gombrich: *The Story of Art*, p. 20.
3. E. B. Tylor: *Anthropology*, Chapter 13, "Science."
   K. Birket-Smith: *Geschichte der Kultur*, Chapters 3, 4, 5.
4. R. W. Frith: "Magic." In: *Encyclopaedia Britannica*, Vol. XXIV, 1971, p. 572.
5. B. Malinowski: *Magic, Science and Religion*, (1948), Chapter 5, paragraph 5. This is a modified view on magic as presented originally by Tylor and Frazer who then called magic an "ineffective substitute for science," this formulation having later been discarded altogether.
   E. B. Tylor: *Primitive Culture*, (1871).
   J. G. Frazer: *The Golden Bough*, (1922), Chapter 4, "Magic and Religion."
6 R. W. Frith, *op. cit.*
   B. Malinowski: *Magic, Science and Religion*, Chapter 1.
7. B. Malinowski: *Magic, Science and Religion*, Chapter 5, paragraph 6.
8. B. Malinowski: *Coral Gardens and their Magic*.
9. F. Boas: *Primitive Art*, pp. 2–3.
10. J. G. Frazer, *op. cit.*, Chapter 4, "Magic and Religion."
11. E. H. Gombrich: *The Story of Art*, Chapter 1, "Strange Beginnings."
12. F. Boas: *Primitive Art*, Preface, p. 1.
13. *Ibid.*, p. 346.
14. W. Wundt: *Völkerpsychologie*, Vol. III, Die Kunst, 3rd ed.
15. F. Boas: *Primitive Art*, p. 12.
16. K. Moszyński: *Człowiek*, p. 572.
17. M. Sobolewska-Drabecka: "Niektóre zagadnienia z najdawniejszych dziejów tańca." In: *Swiatowit*, Vol. XXIII, (1960), pp. 87–112.
18. A. H. Brodrick: *Prehistoric Painting*.
19. Stiegelman: *Altamira*.
    L. Frobenius and D. C. Fox Douglas: *Prehistoric Rock Pictures in Europe and Africa*.
    H. Kühn: *The Rock Pictures of Europe*.
20. Marques de Lozoya: *Historia del Arte Hispanico*.
21. E. O. James: "Prehistoric Religion." In: *Man and His Gods*, p. 27.
22. *Ibid.*, p. 27.
23. A. Lommel: *Prehistoric and Primitive Man*, p. 16.
24. M. Eliade: *Shamanism*, p. 459.
25. D. Lévi-Strauss: *Totemism*.
26. E. Tylor: *Primitive Culture*.
27. R. R. Marett: *The Threshold of Religion*.
28. H. Breuil: *Les Peintures Rupestres Schématiques de la Péninsule Ibérique*, Vol. IV.
29. *E.g.* in South Africa until 1820–70, the time of the arrival of Europeans; in the Drakensberg Mountains, depicting British soldiers. (A. Lommel: *Prehistoric and Primitive Man*, p. 23).
    D. S. Davidson: "Aboriginal Australian and Tasmanian Rock Carvings and Paint-

ings." In: *Memoirs of the American Philosophical Society*, Vol. V, Philadelphia, (1936).

C. P. Mountford: *Aboriginal Paintings from Australia.*

Unesco World Art Series: Australia—Aboriginal Paintings—Arnhem Land.

D. Bleek, E. Rosenthal, A. J. H. Goodwin: *Cave Artists of South Africa.*

J. D. Lajoux: *Rock Paintings of Tassili.*

30. E. O. James, *op. cit.*, p. 23.

31. A. L. Godlewski: *Kultury zbieracze i lowieckie*, pp. 40–41.

C. G. and B. Z. Seligmann: *The Veddas*, pp. 209–72.

32. P. Schebesta: *Bei den Urwaldzwergen von Malaya.*

33. O. Schebesta: *Die Bambuti; Pygmäen vom Ituri.*

34. L. Marshall: "The Kung Bushmen of the Kalahari Desert." In: J. L. Gibbs (ed.): *Peoples of Africa.*

35. O. Schellong: "Musik und Tanz der Papuas." In: *Globus*, Vol. IV, no. 6.

36. J. D. Woods (ed.): *The Native Tribes of South Australia.*

37. C. Darwin: *Voyage of the Beagle.*

M. Gusinde: *Die Feuerland Indianer.*

38. G. P. Kurath: "Native Choreographic Areas of North America." In: *American Anthropologist*, pp. 55 (1): 60–73.

39. J. G. Frazer, *op. cit.*, p. 65.

40. *Ibid.*, p. 71.

41. M. Eliade: *Patterns in Comparative Religion.*

42. J. G. Frazer, *op. cit.*, p. 72.

43. G. Parrinder: *Man and His Gods*, p. 15.

E. E. Evans-Pritchard: *Theories of Primitive Religion*, p. 101.

M. Douglas: *Purity and Danger*, (1970), p. 74.

44. M. Eliade: *Patterns in Comparative Religion*, p. xii, pp. 4–7.

45. E. Bourguignon: *Trance Dance*, pp. 9–19.

46. *Ibid.*, pp. 15–16.

S. Wavell, A. Butt, N. Epton: *Trances.*

47. A. Rouhier: *La plante que fait les yeux émerveillés.* About peyotl used in Mexico during religious festivals. This practice is found especially among South American Indians and some North Asiatic peoples, E. Bourguignon, *op. cit.*, p. 12.

48. K. Birket-Smith, *op. cit.*, pp. 297, 303, 338, 344, 417, 420, 451.

49. Beck: *Die Ecstase*, p. 79.

50. E. Bourguignon, *op. cit.*, p. 15.

51. Laurens van der Post, a talk on BBC 1 (British television), 7th September, 1969: "The Awakening Spirit."

52. E. and L. Selenka: *Sonnige Welten*, p. 133.

53. H. Werner: *Einführung in die Entwicklungspsychologie*, p. 262.

54. Beck, *op. cit.*, p. 79.

55. E. Bourguignon, *op. cit.*, p. 15.

56. M. Eliade: *Shamanism; Archaic Techniques of Ecstasy.*

Lommel: "Der Schamanismus." In: *Naturvölker in unserer Zeit*, p. 17.

57. F. Andes: "Die Himmelreise der caräibischen Medizinmänner." In: *Zeitschrift für Ethnologie*, Vol. LXX, nos. 3–5, (1939), pp. 331–72.

58. M. Eliade: *Shamanism; Archaic Techniques of Ecstasy*, pp. 29, 73, 128, 143, 164, 243, 305, 312, 340, 344–46, 448–51, 458–59, 460–61, 467–69.

W. Sieroszewski: "Du chamanisme d'après les croyances des Yakoutes." In: *Revue de l'histoire des religions*, Vol. XLVI, (1902).

A. Friedrich: "Knochen und Skelett in der Vorstellungswelt Nord-Asiens." In: *Wiener Beiträge zur Kulturgeschichte und Linguistik*, Vol. IV, p. 225.

H. Petri: "Traum und Trance bei den Australoiden." In: *Naturvölker in unserer Zeit*, p. 31.

59. E. Bourguignon, *op. cit.*, pp. 14–15.
60. H. Webster: *Primitive Secret Societies*, p. 172.
    P. Verger: *Les Dieux d'Afrique.*
61. E. Bourguignon, *op. cit.*, p. 28.
    H. Courlander: *The Drum and the Hoe, Life and Lore of the Haitian People.*
62. B. de Zoete and W. Spies: *Dance and Drama in Bali.*
63. T. S. Raffles: *The History of Java*, p. 340.
    Th. B. van Lelyveld: *La Danse dans le Théatre Javanais.*
    E. and L. Selenka: *Sonnige Welten*, p. 133.
64. J. Moura: *Le Royaume du Cambodge.*
    G. Groslier: *Danseuses Cambodgiennes.*
    R. Cogniat: *Danses d'Indochine.*
    S. Marechal: *Danses Cambodgiennes.*
    C. V. T. Samdach: *Danses Cambodgiennes.*
    W. Ridgeway: *The Dramas and Dramatic Dances of the Non-European Races.*
65. G. Parrinder: *Man and His Gods*, p. 21.
66. L. J. Bertram: "The Origins of Drama." In: *Encyclopaedia Britannica*, Vol. VII, p. 628.
    W. Ridgeway, *op. cit.*, pp. 338, 371, 384–85.
67. L. E. Backman: *Religious Dances in the Christian Church and in Popular Medicine.*
    L. Spence: *Myth and Ritual in Dance Game and Rhyme.*
68. C. M. Bowra: *Primitive Song*, p. 262.
69. W. Ridgeway, *op. cit.*
70. After Burmese scholar, Mr. Taw Sein Ko, quoted in W. Ridgeway, *op. cit.*, p. 257.
71. A. Daniélou: *Bharata Nātyam.*
    A. Daniélou and K. Vatsyayan: *Kathākali.*
    R. Devi: *Dance Dialects of India.*
    B. V. Narayanaswami Naidu, P. Srinivasulu Naidu, O. V. Rangayya Pantulu: *Tāndava Laksanam or the Fundamentals of Ancient Hindu Dancing.*
72. W. Ridgeway, *op. cit.*, p. 156.
73. J. Moura, *op. cit.*, vol. II, pp. 167–68.
74. W. Ridgeway, *op. cit.*, pp. 268, 371.
    Kalvodová-Sis-Vaniš: *Chinese Theatre*, p. 26.
75. *The Fisherman's Revenge* (a Peking opera), pp. 6–7.
76. M. Gunji: *Buyo; the Classical Dance*, pp. 81–82.
77. M. Togi: *Gagaku; Court Music and Dance*, p. 120.
78. Y. Nakamura: *Noh; the Classical Theatre*, p. 56.
79. Y. Toita: *Kabuki; The Popular Theater*, p. 10.
80. W. Ridgeway, *op. cit.*, p. 10.
81. E. Tripp: *The Handbook of Classical Mythology*, p. 203.
82. L. B. Lawler: *The Dance in Ancient Greece*, p. 76.
83. Aristotle: *Poetics*, 1449, A, 9–15.
84. W. Ridgeway, *op. cit.*, pp. 3–4.
85. R. Laban: *Mastery of Movement*, p. 3.
86. L. E. Backman, *op. cit.*
87. E. Bourguignon, *op. cit.*, pp. 10–11.
88. L. Backman, *op. cit.*
    J. A. M. Meerloo: *Dance Craze and Sacred Dance.*
89. A. Lommel: *Prehistoric and Primitive Man*, p. 8.
90. B. Gunda: "Die mitteleuropäischen Bauernkulturen und die Methode der 'Cultural Anthropology'." *VIᵉ Congrès International des Sciences Anthropologiques et Ethnologiques, Paris, 1960.* Musée de l'Homme, Paris, (1963), p. 543, 2:1.

91. T. Shanin (ed.): *Peasants and Peasant Societies.*
92. R. Lange: "Traditional Dances of Poland." In: *Viltis*, Vol. XXIX, no. 1, May (1970), pp. 4–14; "Der Volkstanz in Polen." In: *Deutsches Jahrbuch für Volkskunde*, Vol. XII, (1966), Part 2, pp. 342–57.
93. M. Arnaudoff: *Die Bulgarischen Festbräuche*, pp. 50, 54.
94. The *Guardian*, 22nd May, 1972.
95. The *Guardian*, 22nd May, 1972.
96. V. von Plessen: "Bei den Flussvölkern von Borneo." In: *Atlantis*, Vol. VIII, (1936), p. 660.
97. E. Bourguignon, *op. cit.*, pp. 9, 19.
    H. Jeanmaire: *Dionysos; Histoire du Culte de Bacchus.*
    E. de Martino: *La Terra del Rimorso.*
98. J. Henney: "Trance Behaviour among Shakers of St. Vincent." Working Paper No. 8, *Cross-Cultural Studies of Disassociational States*, Columbus, Ohio, (1967), pp. 6, 9.
    E. Bourguignon, *op. cit.*, p. 21.
99. J. Mooney: *The Ghost Dance Religion and the Sioux Outbreak of 1890.*
100. E. Bourguignon, *op. cit.*, p. 24.
101. E. Bourguignon, *op. cit.*, p. 22.
102. M. Buber: *Die Erzählungen der Hassidim*, pp. 25, 134, 286–87, 333, 545–46, 550–51.
103. J. E. Harrison: *Ancient Art and Ritual.*
104. A. Lommel: *Prehistoric and Primitive Man*, p. 13.

Chapter 7

How Dance Functions and the Forms it Takes

If we are to consider man's capacities in dance, we ought to start analysing the dance activities of a single person. We have here again to be reminded that the instrument of the dance is the dancer's body itself. Therefore, the limits of any dance structure are strongly conditioned by the anatomical possibilities of the human body; hence the universality of basic dance structures among all human beings.

The main movement units employed are steps, jumps, turns, and arm, leg, head, and trunk gestures. Many transitional states are possible, such as the partial supporting of the body, where only part of the body weight is used. Also gliding movements may appear as a complementary feature.

The body moving in space instantly projects congruous shapes because it is a functional structure itself. This, however, is enriched by the addition of the dancer's personal range of capacities in using his movement. These he may employ in dance in many different ways. As a result, many combinations of movement qualities come into play:

— to "project" the movement generally out of the body or into it (Free and bound flow, after Laban — an element of control allows the movement freely out of the body, or binds it to it in relation to the body centre.)

— to explore the manifold relationships of different body parts to each other in motion. (How many parts or counterparts of the body are in action; the way they move in relation to each other — in unison or following different rhythms; which body part is dominant — torso, arms, legs, etc.)

— to expose the movement structure in dance externally or to keep it restricted to the minimum. (Sometimes the minimum expansion is sufficient in building up a dance form for one's own dancing. The dance is in this case self-contained and not explicitly directed to the spectator. In dances orientated to the audience the movement expansion often increases and the shapes become exaggerated.)

— to establish different relationships to the ground. (A dancer may have the general tendency to direct his action "into the ground," parallel to it, or away from it. This refers to the "low," "medium," and "high" type of dancing as proposed by Laban.)

— to use the space surrounding the dancer in different ways. The main divisions are: dancing on the spot or travelling away. (There may be, for example, sitting dances or dances exploring different floor patterns.)

— to reveal the relationships to ideas and thoughts as made possible through the idiom of movement. (The dance structures, when exposing some content, become meaningful shapes. They take on more or less abstracted symbolic features. These are recognisable through their common movement expression, or they acquire secondary, conventional meaning.)

It is out of these many interrelationships that the dynamic content of dance results.

Dance as an art includes all those movement manifestations which take us above the everyday-life level. This may be achieved in different ways, varying in different times and places. As soon as there is no direct biological justification for dancing, another justification is evident. This is the spiritual element which takes over (*see* Chapter 5), and changes the function of movement.

Those movement structures that become meaningful shapes, acquiring the status of symbols, contribute to the outcome of forms which constitute the dance on the art level. But we may already observe the utmost differentiation in the performance of dance forms by different individuals. Here the personal traits become discernible, giving additional characteristics to the movement employed. These secondary characteristics included in a dance structure produce a *personal version* of a dance. This may best be seen in the way the same dance composition is executed by different dancers.

A *style* results from the choice of the dancer in stressing some of the dance components to a greater or lesser degree, and in arranging their proportional display accordingly. The personal style of single dancers is only the exponent of a dancing style that is valid for a particular group of people, nation or school, and this is always culturally conditioned. Even dances that are completely improvised reveal at the same time some stereotype movement sets "owned" by the social group in question. This is because the individual is socially conditioned. He may, however, be unaware that he is executing movement forms which are specific to his group.

It has to be stressed that the art of dance always acquires some form, even in the most tumultuous improvisation. Therefore, one should not try to identify the many possible forms in dance with those few restricted structures as pursued in the urbanised European civilisation. Dance form is not only confined to the formations, or dance elements and motifs, of structural significance. The dance form also encompasses the whole set of attitudes of the dancer. Thus it may include many features, depending on the meanings exposed in it.

Much freedom may be observed in the dancing of "primitive" peoples and peasants, and it is, only after accustoming oneself to their conventions that the rules become evident. These may take on many different manifestations. In this light many "accidental" motions, accents, cries have an entirely different significance as valid components and not as intruders, as some authors try to indicate, in the complexity of a given dance culture.[1]

We have in mind here the manifold appearances of dance in human life, ranging from the spontaneous action caused by mood and resulting in improvisation, to the strictly formed dance where the mood is created solely through the structural content. As long as dance has something to transmit through its own medium it certainly belongs to art in the widest sense of this word.

There is a vast range of degrees between the purely formal and purely emotional approaches possible in the exploration of dance.[2] They usually combine together in a balanced

Plate 54 (*above*): Indians celebrating a hunting festival. The Bororo tribe, Brazil.
Plate 55 (*below*): Suya Indians dancing, Brazil.

Plate 56 (*above*): the "Kolo," circle dance, Slavonia, Croatia.
Photo: M. Pavič, Služba Hrvatske
Plate 57 (*below*): a village dance, Florina, Macedonia, 1962.
Photo: D. Stratou

Plate 58 (*left*): dance of the angels, "Mystic Nativity" by S. Botticelli.
Reproduced by courtesy of the Trustees, the National Gallery, London

Plate 59 (*below*): Israelis dancing on Mount Meron at Lag B'omer, festivities at the tomb of the Rabbi Shimon Bar Yochai.
Photo: Israel Press and Photo Agency

Plate 60 (*above*): joyful dancing following the lighting of the first Hanukka candle on the 4th December at the Western Wall.
Photo: Israel Press and Photo Agency
Plate 61 (*below*): men dancing, Bulgaria.
Photo: Bulgarska Fotografia

Plate 62 (*left*): two-storey circle performed in a churchyard, Ukraine.

Photo: Die Österreichisch– Ungarische Monarchie in Wort und Bild, Galizien, (1898), p. 437

Plate 63 (*right*): two-storey circle, Montenegro.
Photo: Revija, Beograd

Plate 64 (*right*): two-storey dance, Kulu Valley, central Himalayas.
Photo: R. Panjabi

Plate 65 (*right*): wedding dance at Kučkovo, near Skopje, Macedonia, 1940.
Photo: L. S. Janković, Etnografski Muzej, Beograd

Plate 66 (*above*): wedding dance, Beli Potok, near Beograd, 1955.
Photo: Jugo-Foto, Beograd
Plate 67 (*below*): men's kolo, Macedonia.
Photo: Muzikoloski institut Srpska akademija nauka, Beograd

Plate 68 (*above*): Rela dance, India.
Photo: Vijaya photos

Plate 69 (*below*): the "Murrungurru," a traditional welcoming dance, Wailbri tribe, Northern Australia.
Photo: M. Jansen, Australian Information Service

Plate 70 (*above*): women of Netche Village dancing the "Ainilis," a traditional tribal dance of Mare, Loyalty Islands, Melanesia.
Photo: Carolina Photo
Plate 71 (*below*): a Karamojong dance, Karamoja, Northern Uganda.
Photo: A. Gregory

Plate 72 (*right*): clog dancers from North Mara near Lake Victoria, Tanganyika.
Photo: S. Turner
Plate 73 (*below*): men dancing; Xingu, Brazil.
Photo: R. Hanbury-Tenison

Plate 74 (*above*): warriors dance, Assam, India, 1958.
Photo: UNESCO/G. Mehta
Plate 75 (*below*): the "Kailao," war dance, 'Uvea, Polynesia.
Photo: P. Sergi

Plate 76: the "Kailao," war dance, 'Uvea, Polynesia. Dancers divided into two parties.
Photo: P. Sergi

Plate 77: traditional "Dance of the Old Man," Mexico.
Photo: B.G. Silberstein

Plate 78 (*above*): "Ula," an old dance performed by maidens, Tonga, Polynesia.
Photo: P. Sergi
Plate 79 (*below*): the "Maa'ulu'ulu," a sitting dance, Tonga, Polynesia.
Photo: P. Sergi

Plate 80 (*right*): dancers of the Dinka tribe, South Sudan.
Photo: M. M. Ninan
Plate 81 (*below*): tribal dancing in the desert, Northern Africa.
Photo: E. G. Schwab

Plate 82: the "Šedlácká," a couple dance, Moravské Slovacko.
Photo: ČSAV, Brno

Plate 83: a picture of a peasant couple dancing, area of Cracow, Poland, early nineteenth century.
Biblioteka Zakladu Ossolińskich, Wroclaw

Plate 84: quadrille danced by young people in their grandparents' clothes, French Pyrenees.
Photo: H. Cartier-Bresson

Plate 85: the "Trojok," dance for three, Silesia, Poland, 1973.
Photo: P. Sobczyński

arrangement. If, however, one or another is over-exposed it usually results in failure. Thus, if the dance loses its content and retains only the empty structure it does not transmit anything; for instance there are "folk dances" that repeat only the shape, having lost the motivation entirely. The same may be true of a dance containing ideas and emotions, but without the necessary support of an intelligible structure; for instance, there can be self-indulgent improvisation which does not conclude in any dance form.

The dancer on his own may first of all perform some dance-like movements spontaneously as the result of increased emotional tension, (emotional tension resulting in motor activities). This is often particularly true with children or young individuals. Primarily it is connected with the biological function, and is discussed at length in Chapter 4. In these "dances" particular shapes are employed but their arrangements are not consciously selected.

During my fieldwork (1954–67) in Eastern Europe, I sometimes came across girls "dancing for themselves" whilst guarding the cattle. This was conditioned by the isolation of the young shepherdesses who spent many lonely days in the pastures. These young girls had little time to join the village dances. Only when still children would they have had the chance to look through the windows of the village dwellings and see the dances of the adults inside. They found some compensation in their improvised dances.

But altogether a dancer performing on his own is a rarity in human culture. Man is a gregarious being and, as such, is used to receiving confirmation of his actions. If he dances in seclusion it is usually a spontaneous outlet for his stresses. In intended improvisation a response or counterplay with other human beings is already expected.

As soon as the single person takes on a special mission, the action becomes ritualised and, as a result, the dance acquires formal features, *e.g.* the shaman going into trance, possession dances with special "steps," particular postures and facial expressions when different spirits are personified, or the whirling dance movements of the dervishes or Hassidim performed to achieve a state of intoxication for religious purposes. The dance movements as executed by priests in different epochs also reveal set patterns transmitting symbolic meaning. These dance forms are inherited by the following generations as part of their cultural equipment.

A ritualised dance movement is always directed to a receiver. This might be a deity, another participant or a spectator. The shaman or magician, even when achieving the state of trance, must still follow the prescribed ritual dance form. Only in this way can the message be received by the participants and understood by the spirits. If, for example, the dance is performed in the "wrong" way, it has to be started again.[3]

In some instances, the dancers may form a *shapeless group*. This is usually the result of an accidental outburst of dance activity or involvement in possession trance (for example, the Kris dancers in Bali at the moment when they turn the daggers against themselves), when every dancer is concerned only with his own spiritual experience. Each dancer performs his own dance following a different movement concept and a different rhythmic background. It is, as it were, a multiplication of many single dances without any link uniting or organising them into a joint action. The only common elements here are the unity of place and time of execution.

Sometimes the same rhythmic background may be provided but different individual movement versions executed (for example, the dances of the Vedda tribes around the arrow).[4] This already organises the group action to a greater extent, but still in a very limited way.

Only a common movement theme has the property of completely unifying a group in its dance activity. In order to be able to follow the same dance idea, the rhythmic background has to be externalised, thus the clapping and beating of drums, etc. are necessary to provide the same time organisation for every dancer. But first of all the movement shape forming the dance theme must be known. In this way, everybody joins the same dance form, thus strengthening the dynamic force of the dance activity.

The dance form will also depend on the relationships created in a group situation — of the dancers to each other and of the dancers to the surrounding space.

The spatial arrangements resulting from these relationships produce shapes and specific *formations*. This produces, in turn, a *shaped group* in dance activities. Here, the desires of the individual are coupled with the aims of the group to which he belongs. Needless to say, an organised group dance may become a powerful factor in strengthening social bonds. A group feels stronger if united by an idea, and this is an important factor for a human group facing the problems of living at different times. It also produces collective responsibility, the individual being dissolved into the whole group's doings. This allows an intensity of action to build up to a far greater height than could ever be attained by one individual acting alone. These features are easily induced by dance. That is why the major role of dance in organising the human community, from the earliest stages of history onwards, is so often explored by the magician, shaman, leader, etc.

The ideal dance form for this is the *circle*. In it, all the dancers are on equal terms in relation to the centre of the circle and to each other. Everybody has the same distance from the centre and has a partner either on his right and left or in front and behind. This contributes to the promotion of unified mood and action.

In some dances, the participants progress on their own in the circle without holding each other. The closed character of a circle (or any other formation), however, is strengthened by different ways of holding each other. This may be done by holding hands, putting arms on the partner's shoulders, crossing arms before holding, holding the ears of the neighbours (New Guinea, Greece),[5] holding the belts of the partners or even by locking little fingers (*e.g.* Bretagne gavotte).[6]

As soon as the circle moves, everyone has to apply his own movement capacities to the required interpretation which is functionally conditioned by the dance's structure. Only then is the participant able to fit into the dance faultlessly. Otherwise he will have difficulty in keeping within this particular dance form. This does not mean that no improvisation is admitted. I very well remember seeing a circle dance (Koleso) performed by girls in the village of Lipnik Maly (Slovakia) in 1961. They started their dance in the circle with a "sidestep-close" repeated for a long time. Once the feeling of unified action was established, one of the girls suddenly burst out with an improvised song. This finally led the whole circle into a whirlwind-like movement around the central focus. After it had "run out" they returned to the slow "step-close" action again, so establishing their base for another improvised song, which led once more into the incredible speed of the dance.

The centre of the circle is the focus, of which the dancers are very aware. All the dance action is applied to it and choreo-technically the centrifugal force is often used, enabling the dancers to go around more easily. This promotes the feeling of unity and elation to a further degree.

It is only when teaching a circle dance to people from cultural areas where this dance form was long ago forgotten that one becomes aware of the special attitude required to be able to join in this type of dance. The centre of the circle is the natural point of attention, and for this reason it has been used so very often as the site of the symbol around which the dance takes place, *e.g.* a fire, killed animal, offering, altar, newly-wed couple, maypole, etc.

Most of the circle dances are therefore connected in a natural way with magical and social functions. The closed circle stresses also very much that the outside world is excluded. It is protective, not allowing alien forces to penetrate into the enclosure. It also takes the group out of the surrounding environment in the most ideally organised way. All the dancers' intentions and actions are absolutely unified.

Sometimes it may be found that owing to shortage of space and great numbers of participants (*e.g.* the whole village taking part), the outlines of a circle may become blurred. This is not disturbing as long as the tempo of the dance is not too fast. In faster circular dances, the shape of the circle will be even because of the way this form functions choreotechnically.

Occasionally one may come across several concentric circles in a dance. These may in addition move in opposite directions around the same focus.

Sometimes a "double storey" circle is evident — the dancers of the upper circle stand or sit on the shoulders of the lower one (*e.g.* Ukraine, Jugoslavia, Caucasia).[7]

Two basic directions of circling are possible (clockwise and anti-clockwise). In some cultures it is "right" to dance in one way, in other cultures it is the opposite. In some cases, the "wrong" direction taken may be considered as a mistake or may even be thought dangerous. In some cultures again, the direction of circling has no significance whatsoever.[8]

As soon as the circle *opens up*, there is a fundamental change in the situation. When moving in any of the basic directions one of the dancers at the extreme edge becomes a leader. Sometimes he may have his own part, which may be improvised, and a *chain* of dancers follows him.

The opening of the circle creates an entirely different atmosphere. There is nothing more to be excluded from the circle or protected inside it. The stress is on progression rather than on dancing around one focus. The leadership of the furthest dancer allows him to take the group out of the strict circle formation and results in forms such as the spiral and the serpentine.

The function of the leader also enables the group to be transferred to a different place. This may be a convenient form for reaching an aim of special significance. The result of this is the *processional* type of dancing.

The processional form is entirely concerned with progression over the dance surface. Therefore, the arrangements are different. The forward step is here more relevant than the side step of the open circle or chain.

A *line* of people side by side as a dance form again introduces a different attitude of the dance group. There is something to be faced, met or fought against if necessary. For example, most of the war dances consist of line formations. Sometimes a multiple line heightens the intensity of the attack.

Two parallel lines facing each other are predestined to be a *dialogue dance*. Indeed, in some instances, whilst the one line is advancing, the other stands and receives the "message." After the retreat of the first line, the other one repeats the same action. This "exchange" of messages is sometimes strengthened by the text of songs which occasionally even contain insults.

Sometimes a dance unit may consist of *two dancers* (not yet a couple). An interaction of the two may be the result; but they do not hold each other and to varying degrees may be independent of each other.

A *couple* as a dance unit is at the same time a micro-formation in itself. The two people move around or alongside their common axis. There are instances when they form a world on their own, concerned solely with their own interaction, and this may be the essence of the given dance.[9]

In the couple formation, however, the most common movement explored is the rotation around the common axis of the partners. This may be done on the spot or whilst whirling on a circle line. This double rotation gives another new facet to dance activities.

If there are many couples joining the dance in this way, the integrity of the whole group comes alive, still leaving room for the integrity of the couple as the smallest unit. The capacity of the circle dance is here re-employed to some extent, except that connections are established between couples instead of between every dancer.

The independent micro-formation of the couple sometimes allows them to execute their own variations (micro-composition), these blending into the general trend of the dance. At the same time, the feeling for the circle formation may be well retained. For example, in some of the Eastern European peasant dances the whirling couples are not expected to enter the interior of the circle. The centrifugal power is employed to a high degree by the group moving in a united way on the circle. This presents a striking contrast to a Western social whirling dance as performed in leisurely manner around the ballroom (*e.g.* the waltz) where there is no demand that the circle be strictly observed.

The dance unit consisting of *three, four, or more dancers* will accordingly have its dance capacities functionally conditioned. The dancers may progress forward, backwards or sideways. Sometimes, if this unit is multiplied, it takes on the form of a processional progression. In some instances, chain dance elements are traceable (*e.g.* Bretagne gavotte). Very often, these dances consist of a combination of different elements. For example, movements forwards and backwards in the first part are complemented by the whirling interchange of every two dancers around their own axis, whilst the third dancer waits without moving, etc.

In addition to these main features of group formations there are many *transitional types* in evidence. Also many more details may be found, thus contributing to the outcome of countless combinations. However, they will all refer more or less directly to the main types (*see* Fig. 6).

The short typological indication given above does no more than to introduce the problem. C. Sachs, in his monumental work on dance, tried to establish a dance typology. He was, however, without success owing to the lack of relevant materials and limited methods applied.

He tried to classify dance forms according to their *structural* elements, and he did not then have sufficient information about their validity in the functioning of dance. Irrelevant and accidental features were often chosen as characteristic symptoms, leading as a result to a very blurred picture of the whole. In line with the approach of the historical school in favour

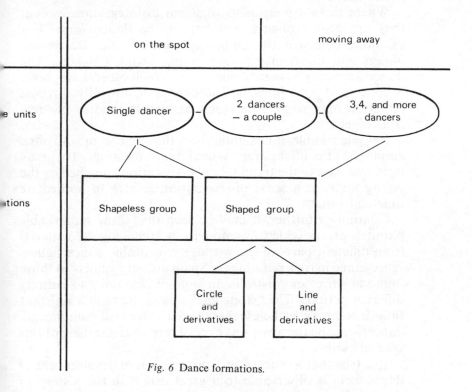

Fig. 6 Dance formations.

at that time, Sachs also tried to establish *absolute chronologies* of dance, showing its development from the simplest to the most complex forms, in historical perspective. This would imply that dance *only* ever developed in one way, and that it has been necessary for all peoples to go through the succession of more and more complex dance forms.

In reality, it seems more probable that the universality of human nature secures a similar response in similar conditions. This is applicable all over the world and throughout the history of mankind. Therefore, it seems impossible to establish any absolute chronological development of dance forms. In similar conditions producing certain social attitudes, similar forms are applied.

Indeed, it seems that where social integration is evident and manifested, a more integrated dance form is applied, (circle, chain, line, etc.).

Where there are elements of social disintegration evident they are also explicitly manifest in the dance form. For example, compare the similarity between the trance-like dances and the contemporary young people's dances. The dancers actually have no connection to each other. Everybody is concerned with himself. The degree of inwardly directed attention may sometimes reach paranatural states of "real trance," etc.

It is remarkable, for example, how the circle form is so often employed at contemporary Israeli dance meetings. This may be in response to the trend for collectivisation launched by the young State, as a sense of integration is here of immediate practical value.

Continuing further, it may be seen that some remarkable parallels are provided by comparing archeological material from different parts of the world, *e.g.* neolithic dance figures represented in rock paintings of Spain are very similar to those found in Africa or Australia, in spite of belonging to entirely different periods. The "stone age" existed there in a different time. It seems nevertheless that the dance form of "supplicant" dancers raising the arms was everywhere characteristic of this type of culture.

It is true that a "successive" progression of development of dance form is observable to a great extent in the history of dance in Europe, (*e.g.* from circle, line, chain to couple dancing and disintegrated forms). But one easily forgets that this may simply be mirroring certain stages of social attitudes characteristic only of the history of European civilisation. Similar dance forms may have been employed in other cultures throughout history, but the order may have been different, varying in response to the particular social development of the people concerned.

Much more well-guided research and professionally collected and documented dance material is needed, however, to tell us about the existing relationships between the dance forms and their functions, and the extent to which they mirror specific features of the cultures to which they belong.

REFERENCES

1. F. Boas: *Primitive Art*, p. 346.
2. *Ibid.*, p. 13.
3. C. G. and B. Z. Seligmann: *The Veddas*, p. 265.
4. *Ibid.*, p. 214.
5. C. Sachs: *The World History of the Dance*, p. 144.
6. J. M. Guilcher: *La Tradition populaire de danse en Basse-Bretagne*, p. 149.
7. L. S. and D. S. Jankovic: *Folk Dances*, Vol. I, III and IV (Hercogovina, Montenegro).
8. C. Sachs: *World History of the Dance*, pp. 147–48.
9. Z. Jelìnková: *Tóčivé tance*; "Drehtänze." In: *Journal IFMC*, Vol. XV, (1963), p. 167.

Chapter 8

Dance—a Component of Human Culture

Dance represents a primeval component of culture and shows many universally human features, being valid throughout the whole history of mankind right down to our own times. In spite of technological progress, we still dance in our contemporary, urbanised world. Dance is still of relevance to us — it is still needed in our culture.

However, the significance of dance in human culture varies, depending upon the degree to which social bonds are maintained. These are usually strongest in places or areas of local self-sufficiency. Isolation from the "outside" world is maintained, sometimes no class division is evident.

The pace of life under these conditions is applied organically, allowing sufficient time for impressions to be processed. Therefore, the most extensive application of dance is contemporarily found only among "primitive" and old peasant cultures which have a highly integrated social structure.

In spite of being inferior to the mature cultures in respect of their material, economic and technological development, "primitive" and "retarded" cultures often surpass them in their artistic achievements.[1]

The direct way in which "primitive" man perceives his environment, and the direct way he manifests his ideas, are at the root of the freshness of "primitive" art and its deep relevance to life. Here dance is the great art because of its primary properties (*see* Chapters 4 and 5).

Fundamentally, the communicative characteristics of dance are employed: the contagious spell of dance movement comes into play. This is heightened by the simultaneous participation of the whole community in the dance.

Let us now consider the different instances when the dance may take on special functions in human culture.

First of all the recreational value of dance has been explored to different degrees all through the ages. Dance was undoubtedly the main entertainment of the camp, settlement and village in the past, although certainly in a different way from that which is understood in an urbanised society.

In the old type of village life, dance was a necessity, an organic part of the group's functioning. It was not an optional adornment or staged performance. In group dances, a community primarily gains the feeling of togetherness. In the early stages of human development, among existing "primitive" populations, and still surviving where the social ties are maintained, dance is particularly a necessary and integral part of community life and takes on many social functions, sometimes closely connected with customs and rites. Indeed, for some peoples dance is the main means of organisation.[2]

Thus the serious role dance plays in human culture in this instance can be seen. When acquiring a special function, the dance shape is accordingly adjusted. The easily-found symbolic elements in dance are employed to make the action meaningful, different, and unusual.

Sometimes a dance develops a special pattern for ritual purposes. Sometimes one of the dance types takes on the ritual function temporarily.

Special dances leading to ecstatic states are used in many instances and for different purposes by magicians, priests and leaders in actions designed to induce mass psychosis.[3] In this way, a group can be united in a feeling of deep communion with each other, leading to a liberation from the bonds of individuality, as in the very practical example of preparation before going into battle.

Sometimes dances of this type are used as a sort of group psychotherapy,[4] in which communal exultation produces a release of psychic tensions. This was the means of the oldest types of medicine and was used by medicine men, shamans and priests. Mass suggestion was helpful in curing diseases; thus in "primitive" societies dance was very often used in conjunction with healing treatment.

The same idea was actually maintained by the Ancient Greeks in the Dionysiac dance frenzies, these apparently having a reviving and healing property, and inducing rejuvenation and greater vigour.[5]

These are the reasons why dance, religion and medicine appear together at the dawn of civilisation.[6]

Still closer to our times, in the European Middle Ages, religious dance frenzies broke out (*see* Chapter 6). These dances were supposed to heal people suffering from some sort of epileptic ailment, which may have been caused by ergot poisoning.[7] There is some probability that healing properties were received in performing the monotonous and exhausting dance steps in such religious processions.

Also, not so long ago, modern societies experienced dance frenzies connected with hypnotic cures; the Shakers and Jumpers in the nineteenth century can be mentioned here.

Contemporarily, trance dance is still used by many of the South American religious sects in conjunction with healing (*see* Chapter 6). A Brazilian psychiatrist recently obtained positive results when using dance methods of certain cults experimentally in the modern setting of a medical institute.[8] The religious aspects were entirely omitted and the patients had no connection with the cults. This is another objective proof of the psychological power of dance.

But there are instances when dance has been employed as an even more essential aid to the functioning of human society. We may here distinguish between two basic functions of dance: the social and the magical.

Social functions of dance

(a) Having the meaning of a legal act and being the equivalent of a formal ceremony, for example dances connected with initiation, marriage and funerals. These dances stressed the changes occurring in the life of a single person or within a social group.

(b) Stressing the division of the society and the status of the performers — dances reserved for performance by special people.

(c) Stressing the social integration of the village community and allowing it to experience the feeling of togetherness in dances which are performed only for entertainment.

Magic functions of dance

(a) To secure an increase in fertility and good luck.

(b) To chase away evil influences and powers.

Naturally, these divisions are not rigid because very often a magic dance may at the same time have a social function. Indeed, many transitional types are possible.

Generally speaking, while the social functions of dance are concerned mainly with family life and group life organisation, the magic dances are basically concerned with the well-being of the group and its economy, *e.g.* hunting activities, the agricultural cycle, etc. For this purpose sympathetic magic is employed, following the use of analogies. For instance, the higher one jumps, the higher the crops will grow, etc.

I am going to introduce here some selected examples from different areas, but first I would like to give some from Poland, as they are well-known to me and give a good idea about the functioning of dance in an old rural culture.

In the area around Warsaw a custom was known according to which the women used to jump high in the fields, after sowing the hemp, believing that this would strengthen the growth of the plants. From the northern part of Poland on Ash Wednesday the women formed a circle and danced around several times, and at the end of this they would jump over benches. In the northern part of Poland the fertility dances used to be performed for three days and for three nights before Ash Wednesday. To provide continuity, each night's dancers were replaced in the morning by another group. They were not allowed to interrupt the dance. According to local belief, the good quality of the linen was secured in this way.

There were also dances for a good harvest of different crops, for example, in the province of Silesia, for mushrooms, cabbages and potatoes; in the central part of Poland, for oats. In the area around Cracow, the men danced for wheat, the women for hemp and the girls for a magic herb.

Dances following the same principle are found in many places all over the world. For instance, in South-east Australia, the adult members of the Kurnai tribe hold their children high whilst dancing, to make them grow tall.[9] Similar dances used to be performed in Ancient Mexico.[10]

In Western Australia (Watchandi tribe) during the Spring Festival, a semi-religious ritual is performed at night. After the women and children leave, the men dance alone around a hole dug in the ground, accompanying themselves with cries and songs. After a long period of time, as the excitement reaches its peak, they then plunge their spears repeatedly into the hole. This is the symbolic dance of fertility, which must dutifully be observed by the men.[11]

In Western Poland, there still survives a fertility rite called "podkoziołek" (the goat), which includes many crude customary elements. This rite again is connected with dance. On Shrove Tuesday the boys and girls go round the village, visiting all the houses. The boys are dressed in fertility symbols, carrying masks of a goat, horse, bear and stork. Everybody gives them food or money. After this procession is completed, they move to an inn. The collected food is distributed among the participants and a special dance starts. It is unusual, in that during the whole year the boys have to pay for all the music; on this one day, it is the girls only who do so. Each of them will be led separately by her boy to a spot in front of the musicians. A little figure made from potatoes or swedes representing a goat or a nude man is already standing before them. A special ritual song will be performed, and after that the girl has to put her gift of money on a plate in front of the symbol. The musicians play, and each couple performs a short dance, immediately followed by the next couple. It has the meaning of a symbolic marriage for those who have not yet fulfilled their duty in accordance with Nature's laws.[12]

In some parts of Poland the farmer's wife has to dance with a man dressed up in straw as a bear. The hemp will then grow better. This happens mainly on Ash Wednesday.[13]

Once, the practice of naked married women from Anhelow (Ukraine) performing a circle dance during the night was known as a means to further the healing power of herbs.[14]

On St. John's Day in Macedonia[15] everybody joins the kolo for health, life and luck. On that day, the women in mourning sing for the first time.

On this same saint's day, Polish girls in olden times performed a circle dance around the fire, the purpose of which was to chase away the evil powers and to experience the purifying power of fire. The girls made girdles of wormwood for themselves as this was acknowledged as the magic plant giving protection against evil.[16] The people of Macedonia,[17] living at the foot of Jablanica, light great fires on the mountains during the night before Shrove Tuesday, around which people dance all night, giving a welcome to spring.

Also on St. John's Day, the young men and girls from Resan and Prespa (Ohrid area, Macedonia) make a doll "Ivanka" and carry her in a procession. Then they dance all night. This is a rite for good harvest.[18]

At Whitsuntide in Jugoslavia "Kraljıčke igre" (Queen's dances) and customs were performed with ritual or magical purpose. The girl dancers with swords, and the female singers, went in groups from house to house singing and dancing in front of each one for prosperity ("Vojvodina").[19]

"Rusalija" (Macedonia) are dances for health and good harvest, and for healing the diseased. Men dancers come out between Christmas and the Epiphany with wooden swords, attired in ritual dance costume and with ritual gear. Their impressive "slow-motion" actions and steps are to invoke health and healing and a good harvest next autumn. They dance in white costumes with short skirts and use measured sword movements, and are spaced so far apart from one another that each one almost seems to be doing a solo.[20]

The "Lazarice" in Serbia, which are spring dances combined with song, performed by women on St. Lazarus' Day, eight days before Easter, have only recently been taken over by gypsy women who dance for money. The "Kraljice" (Queens) appear on St. George's Day or at Whitsuntide. Their tall, mitre-like head-dresses, often adorned with a sacred picture, make a wonderful show. Originally they carried swords, but later handkerchiefs and fluttering banners of red silk or roughly woven cloth were borne, decorated with apples, bells and magic plants. Their aim, like that of the "Lazarice," is to "bring in" health and happiness.[21]

The Dodole (rain-maids) in Serbia also used to invoke rain and consequent fertility, performing when there was a drought. A group of young girls would go dancing from house to house, singing songs as they went which contained elements of prayers for rain. One of them, the Dodola herself, naked beneath leaves, flowers and green grass, performed alone. The householders would come running out with jars and souse her with water — imitative magic that would assuredly bring rain.[22] To put an end to drought and bring rain, women and girls of the village of Ploska (Russia) sometimes go naked by night to the boundaries of the village and there pour water on the ground.[23]

Among the Omaha Indians (North America), when rain is needed and the corn withering, the members of the sacred Buffalo Society dance around a vessel filled with water. Later they drink the water and spurt it into the air.[24] With the Monumbo–Papua (New Guinea) the masked dancers progress around a water container. After some time, the water is drunk by the women bystanders.[25]

In Serbia, the drought period was caused, according to local belief, by a mythical "serpent," and to chase it away the men assembled in the night and danced naked around the fire. This was followed by a terrifyingly noisy chase through the area, during which the women and children had to hide. (Veliki Izvor, Serbia, 1908.)[26]

The dances of harvest festival all over the world also included many fertility symbols.

For instance, in Polynesia, on the island of Tonga, the field and harvest gods received much attention during both the planting and harvesting activities; and also the rain god used to be appeased to secure enough rain for the fields.[27]

The end of harvesting in the Backa (Vojvodina) was celebrated by a procession, the leader of the harvesters wearing a crown made of ears of corn. It was also celebrated by a kolo, during which the dancers poured water on each other to ensure rain for the next sowing.[28]

In some parts of Poland when the harvest wreath was given by the harvesters to the master after the harvest was completed, the latter was obliged to perform a few simple turns with the first maid. After that the usual dances started.[29]

In the province of Great Poland (Wielkopolska) the farmhands carried these wreaths on their heads while performing a special dance. Afterwards they passed on the wreaths to the girls, who finally carried them to the master. Following this the farmer's wife had to perform a special dance with the chief farm hand. Otherwise, "the crops will not grow next year."[30]

In different parts of Poland (*e.g.* the region of Podlasie) the first maid danced with the last sheaf of corn. Sometimes the girls prepared big straw dolls in the likeness of men and jumped with them in the courtyard (Great Poland). In the latter region a dance existed known as the "Big Father." The farmhands performed it during the harvest festival, and it included high jumps.[31] In the northern part of Poland, the last harvester had to dance first with a straw doll and after that with the farmer's wife.[32]

Among the hunters, animal dances were of course the important feature. They were connected with a formula for luck and divination procured by the shaman; for example the bear dance, performed in the skin of the animal, widespread in Northern Asia (*e.g.* Siberia) and North America[33] (*e.g.* the Iroquois tribe) and also the Yaqui Deer Dance.[34]

Here one also ought to mention the fishermen's dances, *e.g.* in Poland, once performed along the seashore before they went to catch the salmon.[35] They danced around the nets, and this presumably had a magical meaning. The Iroquois and Chippera tribes (America) know very similar fish dances, too.[36]

Sometimes we will find reminiscences of these magic principles present in some of the *family rites*, as for example during the wedding ceremony, funerals, etc. Wedding dances often have a central position in the wedding ceremony. They are the equivalent of a legal act, and additionally they stress the transition from one social group to another, thus the boy is acknowledged as an independent farmer, the girl as a housewife. These ceremonial wedding dances are always performed by people traditionally appointed according to their social status. At the same time, some of the fertility dances, usually performed on other occasions, are incorporated into the wedding rite.

At a Kaffir marriage, singing and dancing is an important part of the ceremony. The relations of the bride and bridegroom dance opposite each other until midnight. The dance's violence increases steadily, leading to improvised leaps and excessive displays of skills. This all has a strong erotic colouring.[37]

The marriage rites at Taveta in East Africa include spasmodic dancing leading to epileptic fits[38] clearly having sexual connotations.

After the wedding in Niš (Serbia),[39] the Kum (best man) cuts off the bride's veil with scissors, and then the couple start the kolo around a fertile tree (initiation). "Šareno oro" (Variegated oro) is the final dance, in which the bride and bridegroom are symbolically joined.

At the beginning of a Macedonian[40] wedding, the mother-in-law (the bridegroom's mother) makes three turns of the "Svekrvino Kolo" (the Mother-in-Law's Kolo) with a sieve on her head, a loaf in the sieve, a jug of wine in her hand, and a pistol in her belt, and with her son, the bridegroom, dancing next to her. At the end of the wedding, the mother-in-law starts the kolo; after her comes her daughter-in-law, and after that her son. Then the bride dances for the first time during the wedding. The wedding ends with the giving of presents to the gypsies (players). At Christmas after the wedding the mother-in-law introduces the young wife into the kolo for the first time.[41]

At Peć (Serbia) kolos are performed around the wedding cake whilst it is being kneaded, around the crepulja (baking cover made of earthenware), or around the hearth whilst the cake is being baked.[42] In Vršac (Vojvodina) the final dance during a wedding is a closed kolo round a fire.[43] In Srem (Vojvodina) the wedding guests, covered with soot, dance at night at the crossroads, while the bridegroom's mother tears a feather cushion into pieces and makes the feathers fly around.[44] In Dubica (Croatia), during the wedding the closed kolo circles around a lit lamp or candle at night.[45]

In the region of Podlasie, Poland, the first wedding dance was introduced by the best man and the bride's mother. Only after that are the other guests allowed to join this brief and special dance. The usual dance festivities follow this introduction.[46]

In one of the south-eastern regions of Poland, the mother of the bridegroom used to receive, as a gift from the bride, a piece of linen woven by her. After capping (ceremony connected with cutting the hair of the bride and putting on a cap — the sign of the married woman) the mother of the bridegroom wrapped herself in this linen and danced a few slow, calm turns with the bride. This was the climax of the whole wedding.[47]

In the eastern region of Podlasie, Poland, the bride approaches each of the guests, bows and invites them to a ceremonial dance. Following this, everybody is obliged to put a coin on the plate held by the bridesmaid. Should anybody not follow this custom, he could easily experience hostility from the crowd, as there exists the deep conviction that this money brings special luck to the young couple. As a rule it is used for buying animals for the new household.[48]

The "Mały taniec" (Little dance) is commonly known all over Poland. In the province of Masovia, for example, the best man dances with the bride after the dinner or after capping. After that, everybody takes several turns with her before she is finally returned to the bridegroom. Before this dance starts, money is collected for the musicians, and then no further payment is made for the music.[49]

Also in the province of Masovia (Mazowsze) the best man guides the bride after the capping in a special Polonaise called "na konopie" for the growth of the hemp.[50] In some parts of the province of Great Poland the bride has to take part in a Shrove Tuesday dance called "do przodka" (Forwards), on this occasion performed only by women. They move in a circle round the bride, and one after the other joins her to turn in the centre.[51]

In another area of the Podlasie region the first dance was customarily always performed by the parents of the bride, holding between them a loaf of bread wrapped in linen.[52]

There are other family rites which include dance as an important element. In Serbia,[53] at the rite of "strižba" (the first cutting of the child's hair) the child's grandparents dance a kolo three times around the child.

Tiv people, a minority group of Nigeria, have dance as a part of their funeral ceremonies.[54] In Poland the old burial rite was often connected with a festive gathering called "stypa" which did not necessarily exclude music and dance. The few reminiscences of ceremonial dance in it, *e.g.* a dance called "pogrzebowy" (the Funeral), recall the original meaning of dance as a means of chasing away death and evil spirits. By performing these special dances, the surviving people were saved from the horror of meeting death.[55] The Manus from New Guinea dance after a period of mourning, to "shake the dust from the house floor."[56]

As previously indicated, although there are great differences between the cultures of "primitive" people and those of "civilised" populations, profound analogies can still be found between them in respect of the basic forms and the social functions of dance. It is indeed astonishing that such deep and genuine connections should still exist. However, the history of the development of European folk-dance, as one possible example, is much more complex, and many infiltrations and adaptations taken from dances of other periods and cultures must be taken into consideration. This is certainly valid to a greater extent with European folk-dance than with the dance of "primitive" cultures.

In the European peasant cultures, there is also evidence of the blending of original magic rites with antique Greek or Roman tradition, plus superimposed Christian elements. Many common features of primarily magic functions may easily be traced, and there are still areas where traditional dance of a certain type is commonly evident in everyday life.

The gap arising between "them" (*e.g.* the "primitive" peoples, the peasants, the common people) and "us" (the urbanised people), is the result of differences in social structures and, following this, in cultural patterns.

One has constantly to remind oneself that in the integrated type of society the various social functions fulfilled by different individuals on certain occasions are not yet specialisations that form a class apart, and as a result, take the individual out of the integral group. Often even the shaman or leader magician, who already has an exposed function, is still estimated as "one of them" and participates in all the remaining activities as any other member of the group.[57]

So dancing as an activity is very much a matter-of-fact occurrence. Everybody joins in it because it is expected in certain circumstances. There is no feeling that it is something done additionally — a superfluous attachment to life which may be omitted without harm being done.

When I was first making beginner's attempts in field-work research, I remember clumsily asking one of my peasant informants, "And what dances do you know?" The logical and slightly impatient answer was: "What do you ask that for? Everybody dances and everybody knows how to dance!" There was no doubt that the villagers would not distinguish between any particular "folk-dances." This idea was already the product of my urbanised environment.

The basic feature of "primitive" dances and dance folklore is that they were created by the dancers for themselves and their own circle, which might include other inhabitants of the same village or other villages, sometimes a great distance away, but always in the same cultural group.

The dance activity in these conditions encompasses everything that is ever danced and, as I was told in the villages to my total amazement, "everything" meant "excluding all that which is not allowed!" But this only becomes clear when one sees the villagers confronted with strange forms. Then these are indeed discarded as "alien," "strange," "not ours," "wrong," etc.

The creator of a dance remains anonymous, although he may sometimes be well-known as a marvellous dancer or as a genuine "ballet-master," and he may enjoy great respect and appreciation. But the production of dance is something entirely natural and is not regarded as a special, independent trade. If there is any specialisation in dance activities, it is still quite different in comparison with dance specialisation in urbanised society.

At some stages, people may only take a passive part in dance, but if they identify themselves fully with the active dancers, they take a real part in the dance activity as a whole. This is again more evident the more the community is socially integrated. In these circumstances, it will also often be difficult to distinguish between pure dance activities and a certain type of dance drama.

Dances that result from relationships between several dancers in action already contain some drama. Moments of drama are sometimes included in magic dances. Also religious drama, as it developed later, is, for the most part, still connected with dance; but here again the spectators are united with the performers in religious activity.

The conscious separation of performers and spectators comes at a later stage, with the specialisation of dance as a performing profession only, and as a form of spectacular entertainment. In this instance, the audience exerts its direct influence on the dance performer from the outside, because "we," the spectators, are always expecting something from "them," the performers.

One of the other basic characteristics of dance in its primary condition is the way in which it is passed on "by word of mouth," the form of the dance being communicated directly from one dancer to another, often being imitated by the receiver.

Of course, dances communicated in this way may undergo some changes in the process of transmission because of the shortcomings of human memory, though it must be remembered that the memory of "primitive" peoples is astonishingly retentive, capable of reproducing incidents from the past, even after a long time, with photographic accuracy. [58] This is one of many factors explaining why traditional dance material is so very conservative. However, this is only true where the cultural balance has not been disturbed abruptly, and the changes that have occurred have evolved slowly and organically.

In some instances, babies are often taken to dance meetings clinging to the bodies of their dancing mothers. Thus it is not surprising that children playing frequently start to imitate the dancing of their mothers and fathers, as they are continually being exposed to dance activities.[59]

Young individuals often attentively watch the adults performing their dances. They are interested because it is only after having passed some form of initiation that they are admitted into the social group of the grown up people, and allowed to join their dances. This is identical with acquiring a new social status.

From ethnographic materials collected in Poland and neighbouring areas, for instance, we know that in some regions the boys and girls were allowed to participate in the whole year's dances only after they had been introduced into the fertility rites on Shrove Tuesday. In other areas, it began with the festive dance performed on St. George's Day. Only after that were they accepted as adults and ready for marriage.[60]

Similarly, almost up to our own times, the debutantes' ball, introducing girls into "society," and the graduation ball, have had a similar function.

The initiation rites of young men and girls occurring among most of the "primitive" peoples actually employ dance as the basic component of the ceremonies.[61] Sometimes the stress is put on the monotonous dances that lead to exhaustion. In this state, the tribal instructions are given to the initiated young men. There are plenty of examples of this among the totemistic cultures of South-east Australia, in large parts of Africa, South-east North America and the Amazon River area, where dance is combined with the use of the totemic ancestors' masks.[62] masks.[62]

Just to add another example, with the Arapaho and Hidatsa Indians (North America), the membership of dance organisations, incorporating all men of the same age, is acquired by learning a particular dance. The instruction is handed on by older men who have already passed through the dance in their day.[63]

But even if some dances are taught to young people, for example during some initiation ceremonies, it is not a dance teacher who does it, but the magician. The dance instruction is centred on the rite rather than on the choreography itself. Dance is here employed only as a means, and its symbolism usually has a magico-religious significance.

From all these circumstances, with dance playing so many roles, one can assume that some details of a dance might not be accurately remembered. The personal element in dance interpretations might also be introduced unconsciously, with the individual interpreter selecting the type of movement best suited to his mood.

Improvisation plays a big part in the creation of dance in these conditions, and in this way new inventions may evolve which will be appreciated intuitively by other dancers and adopted into the traditional repertory. But one should never forget that the criteria in this process, although not written, are very strict. New forms come to life all the time, but the basic style of the components of a dance remain the same, in conformity with very conservative norms.

The dance elements will be improvised on the basis of what is customary in the given period and area. That is why we always find countless variants of the different dances, sometimes even in the area of one village.

In contrast to the dance performances of individuals, in group dances it becomes necessary to emphasise the acoustic background, to organise the time element rhythmically in a unified form perceptible to all participants. Many peoples still do it by clapping, rhythmic shouting, or by reciting words to create rhythmic phrases. As the dance is the main matter, the melodic line of the musical accompaniment is often very poor, and still, even in many European traditional dances, the subordinate role of the music is obvious.[64]

Thus a good deal of music of all kinds developed out of dancing activities. The influence of dance on the shaping of music forms is also evident.[65] Musicologists could have solved many problems concerning some facts on music origins if there had existed concurrently a wider knowledge of dance.

This close interaction between dance and music is still alive even in some parts of Europe. The following example comes from Poland and gives a good idea about this phenomenon. It is a common custom in many areas for the dancer to appear in front of the musicians and to sing to them a chosen dance tune, which is very often improvised as well. After that the musicians take this melody from the dancer and often vary it in the process of playing. The dancer pays his money for it, and with his partner leads the dance as the first couple. The others follow them, dancing around the room. After that another dancer comes with his tune, and in this way the dancing sometimes continues for hours, with short breaks only. If the first fiddler is not capable of catching the melodies given him by the dancers in the manner described above, he may very well literally be chased away and other musicians brought in. Good musicians have a well-established fame, and perform their functions with the greatest dedication. Obviously these musicians play by ear, and none of them can read music.

It is also clear that in this way countless different melodies, even with differences in rhythmic patterns, will be used for the same type of dance.

In the primary conditions, the execution of the dances is closely connected with the musical activities of the people. This feature gets lost in the course of urbanisation. Dance and music become two separate specialisations. Therefore, when for example, trying to reproduce dance folklore outside the original village, basic difficulties arise because of the usual impossibility of providing the interaction of the original music with the spontaneity of the whole dance happening.

Even the use of taped music is of no help in this instance. I remember using music, for a second meeting with dancing villagers, that had been recorded during their dancing the previous evening. To my dismay, they could not dance to it, explaining: "Your music is not following us!"

This is because the musicians have to follow the intentions of the improvising dancers. From their movements they recognise the changes in tempo and the rhythmical variations as introduced by the dancers.

Taking all these characteristics into consideration, one can easily understand that it is much more important, when doing research on a given dance culture, to know the accepted range of a particular style in dance improvisations, than to know the exact description of one accidental variation.

According to this convention, the village names of the different dances cannot help in identifying them; different variants of the same dance may have many different names. Even dances which have a set form may show differences in their interpretations according to the individual or local style.

Thus we see that even the most traditional dance is by no means standardised and static, but is constantly in the process of slow and steady change. There is, therefore, no single uniform pattern for any particular dance, and while this is understandable over a wide territory, it is also evident in a smaller locality, even in a single village.

As a result, some changes arise in traditional dance culture as used by different generations. There are also changes in traditional aesthetic norms, though these are sometimes so gradual as to be almost invisible, the pace of this process depending greatly on outside influences and stimulants.

As dance is not static, but changes in time and territory, let us now take a closer look at the external reasons for these fluctuations.

The nature of the geographical conditions cannot be without influence on the inhabitants of a particular region. For example, there is a difference between the movement patterns of lowlanders living in the plains, and highlanders living in the mountains.[66] Climate also plays a big part, as human psychology is greatly influenced by climatic conditions. In some parts of the world, the climate allows dances to be performed out of doors almost the whole year round, while in other parts this is seldom or never possible. The type of housing may restrict the dance activities, or the type of clothing worn can, for example, restrict the scope of movement. The natural environment determines a people's whole economic background and type of occupation; these in turn condition the way the people move, and so indirectly exert an influence on their dance activities. Therefore, when considering the environment, one has to observe the extent to which man is independent of his conditions; how far he has advanced his technology to rule the environment.

But the main determinant of culture is human society itself. Thus the dance repertory is always shaped to the needs of a given society, and derived from its cultural inheritance. Dance is used by a social group in a particular form, determined by the group's needs and aesthetic norms, and valid for a given period and a given territory. The events of any people's history are of great importance in the development of its dance culture. Such factors as place of origin of the people, the type of government or administration, the alternation of wars and peace, all contribute to shape the traditional dance repertory.

Economic conditions are of importance, too. Whether the particular group of people is rich or poor may be an influential factor in the display of dance activities. In a rich village, for example, a wedding will last for many days, and a full set of musicians will be invited. In a poor settlement, just one musician may provide the music, and the wedding festivities may be reduced to one day only because of shortage of food, etc. Of course, this does not mean that the wealth of a society is the measure of the vigour of its arts — including dance; indeed, the contrary is sometimes true, as the spiritual activities of man are quite independent of his economic conditions.

In poor regions, much more intricacy and inventiveness will frequently be displayed. The best musicians and dancers are very often found among the poor shepherds, serfs in feudal conditions, pastoral people living in hard mountainous conditions, inhabitants of areas with poor soil. A rich area is more often liable to have wider contacts, and to have contact with bigger centres. The people may follow attractive alien examples and become less interested in their own heritage.

What mainly determines the type of culture of a society is its social structure, and this depends largely on its economics. Throughout the whole history of dance we can distinguish roughly between the repertories of the upper and lower classes. Though social restrictions or privileges are often mirrored in dance culture, nevertheless these different repertories very often influence each other, and do not develop entirely independently.

Different dance repertories can also evolve according to a society's division into different social and professional groups. Distinctions can be drawn between the dance repertories of dancers married and unmarried, male and female, etc. and of different groups in specialised work, different professions, grades, etc. We can also distinguish between the world of children and the world of adults in dance.

Still further reasons for changes in dance repertory may be caused directly by:

Migrations of people

Great displacements, sometimes of whole peoples taking their culture with them, may cause dances and dance ideas to be carried to places far away from their original home. But smaller movements of people can produce a similar effect (*e.g.* military service, wars, seasonal work in foreign countries, etc.).

Movement of dance forms without movement of people

There can be a "catching on" and spreading out of an attractive dance form. Many times in the history of dance, observers have noted how contagious some fashionable dance forms are, and how rapidly they spread over large areas of the world, even across national borders and against rulers' prohibitions. If there is a widespread need for a particular type of dance, the dance is quickly taken up by whole populations, sometimes by whole continents, though occasionally the fashionable dance appeals only to some social group or groups of people.

All the above-mentioned factors, contributing to constant changes, are involved in the appearance of *infiltrations* in dance. Any traditional repertory of any cultural group may be influenced by its neighbours or may influence the neighbours' dances. Infiltrations may occur not only between such small territories as regions, counties, etc. but also between whole countries, and not necessarily neighbouring countries. Infiltrations of alien dances into traditional dance repertory may also happen between different social classes (for example, between the aristocracy and the folk, between town and village, between the manor and the peasants, etc.). The prototype may understandably be distorted in this way, primarily because it may be misunderstood and misinterpreted.

But there is a major factor causing the infiltrated dances to change. It is that before these "foreign" dances are incorporated into a traditional repertory, they undergo a process of *adaptation*. They must be "translated", so to speak, into the means of expression used and recognised by the cultural group into which they are received, which may be done quite unconsciously.

The most important feature, so very often ignored by amateur dance collectors and people using the results of their work, is the very congruous character of the traditional repertory. Dances of a particular cultural group, in a particular territory and period, form an organic complex having a clearly established style. Sometimes a dance, or some dances, may be representative of the whole repertory, whilst others remain in the background. Sometimes the main dances of a repertory influence and impart their features to the remaining dances. The dominating dance-types of the repertory usually take on the social and magical functions.

Unfortunately, it is only too often that, when collecting dances, one picks up just one or several "folk-dances," which, after being taken out of their natural context, do not tell us anything about their status in comparison with other dances as used by their original creators and owners. In this way, whole collections of dances lose their value to anyone wanting to know more about the dance's role in the life of a human group.[67] Without knowing their place in the cultural context, we miss the most important element of information: what did these particular dances mean to the people using them? How have they been utilised?

Without respecting these aspects, it will even be impossible to define the general style of dancing in a particular area, etc. This applies especially to places where many dances in the repertory are executed alongside each other. How do we know which of them is the most important if we are only confronted with a list of dances?

From this short review, it will be seen that dance is deeply bound up with human society. Its features are determined by a particular type of culture and, like a living organism, dance is always changing. The dance culture of any society forms a specific complex, and only against this background can it be properly understood.

Dances taken out of their original life context always become something different. Many good examples of this will be found in the way the different European "folk-dances" are used. Taken originally from peasants, and used by the manor-inhabitants or later by townspeople in schools and youth societies or clubs, these "folk-dances" certainly change.

In the case of the European "national dances," many of them became, from the beginning of the nineteenth century, the symbols of patriotic manifestations for entire nations (*e.g.* Hungary, Bohemia, Poland). At the same time, they have been used in this form as a means of recreation or romantically-founded spectacular display. These "folk" or "national" dances certainly differ from their village prototype. The change is even more evident after some of them have been introduced into the theatre (*e.g.* Fanny Elssler dancing the "Cachucha" or the "Cracovienne").

Together with the change of function, there is immediate evidence of the change of form. In some instances, entirely new dances come into existence, if compared with their village prototypes (*see* Fig. 2). Again, they have had to be adapted to the different environment according to its needs. Therefore the original function of these dances, as for example found in the village community, could not be maintained.

This may also happen in many other ways. In the case of children's games and dances, there is a wealth of material taken over by the children from the world of adults. This is a very widespread occurrence.[68]

A few examples from Poland and the Slavic area show convincingly how dances connected originally with the magic function survive as relics in the world of children.[69] Their original function is forgotten as they are used as games, and their original meaning is no longer identified. Many of them are relics of old chain and circle dances, originally so very characteristic of the whole Slavic cultural area.

Some of these games remind us of ancient rites connected with animal sacrifices, as for example the game called "baran" (The ram). Some were connected with spring or summer rites, for example the game called "jawor" (Plane tree) or another one called "mosty" (The bridges). Some of them show well-preserved dialogue dance forms performed with songs. There are also some reminiscences of old wedding rites connected with the buying of the bride. In the province of Małopolska (Little Poland) there is a game called "strzygoń" or "topiec."

Ghosts, spirits of the people, having died a violent death such as by drowning, or for some reason not having found peace, come back to haunt and disturb people. The children try to escape, being haunted in their imagination by these phantoms well-known from folk tales.

Thus a constant change is visible in dance forms as soon as they are taken over from their original owners by a different group of people.

Even the most loving care cannot, therefore, secure the life of dance folklore once it is no longer used in its original surroundings. It is enough to mention as an example the well-organised dance folklore festivals in Strážnice (Czechoslovakia), that have taken place regularly since the Second World War. The villagers have been brought in from remote rural places to display their dances. In the first few years, visitors were still able to meet dance in its genuine peasant form. But soon the same villagers, on returning during succeeding years, became aware of the audiences, and their dances changed accordingly. A new function became dominant, and the dance forms consequently changed. Therefore the struggle to present the execution of authentic folk-dances by outsiders is a sheer impossibility — an illusion.

This does not of course mean that one should not attempt to obtain as authentic dance material as possible. On the contrary, dance as part of cultural heritage should be collected professionally and preserved for future generations. There have been, however, many attempts, in different periods, to "revive" folk-dances, but once cut off from the original source, the dances all inevitably wilt or at least develop into something new, in spite of the organiser's intentions.

All these folk-dance movements, trying to save a national heritage, have undeniably made achievements in their time in many countries of urbanised Europe, serving as a popular means of education. They have often allowed young people to experience dance for the first time, as dance has been lost in many parts of Europe in the course of technological development.

Therefore it is correct to say that there is nothing wrong with dance revivals, as long as it is remembered that in, for example, executing peasant dances, we are not pretending to be peasants ourselves. This also applies, of course, to any type of dance recreated or reconstructed, *e.g.* court dances or ball-room dances of past periods.

The execution of old dance forms gives the opportunity to meet art. Nobody in the civilised world would ever doubt the relevance to contemporary music culture of playing Bach or Mozart. But here we immediately come across the difficulties of interpretation. There is a living tradition of how to interpret, for example, different schools or composers. This is common with all performing arts.

Continuity is necessary in exploring the works of art of the past. This, however, is badly done with dance as there are not enough instructive sources surviving from times when the dances were still alive. Certainly, one is not capable of securing the same sort of original experience in different conditions. At best, as long as it comes alive, it may be a well-revived copy of a dance, and in that form it immediately acquires a new value. But it will never be identical with the original. This is simply a fact, and one has to accept it.

Also even in music, exact reconstructions have sometimes only caused disappointment, because when played on older types of musical instruments (*e.g.* the early piano), the music may no longer conform to the size of our concert halls or the tradition of performing to which we are accustomed, etc. But still the music comes alive, otherwise it would never speak to us. The same is true of dance.

Dance forms an integral part of the self-contained type of life patterns found among peasants and "primitive" peoples, while urban patterns of life do not. We are witnessing contemporarily a rapid crumbling away of these last old cultural reservoirs, as they are suddenly confronted with technological and urbanised civilisation.

As soon as the cultural integrity of a human group splits, the traditional dance becomes lost, because it ceases to retain its vital social significance. The urbanised type of life requires new media, and the intruding new elements cannot be absorbed quickly enough. There is no longer time, place or need to follow the old patterns of dance. Nor may dance respond to the demands of the new situation.

On the other hand, it may be interesting to follow the way urban social dancing is adapted by villagers. When they come into contact with the dances in fashion, these are still inevitably translated into their own medium of dance. To us it may appear funny or clumsy, but if we consider that this is yet another example of adaptation it may prove to be fascinating study material. The transitional type of dance evolving here is often not yet clearly determined. It may best be experienced in the suburban areas of big industrial centres, where the first generation of people live in new conditions that are strange for them. Here once again the unofficial stream of dance culture continues along with the official one accepted by fashion centres, which dictate cosmopolitan social dances.

From our survey on dance throughout this book we are able to recognise that many of the seemingly "primitive" and remote aspects of dance culture still have some relevance in our contemporary world.

First of all, dance requires the involvement of all human faculties. This still applies in our times, if we intend to meet dance as an art. At the same time we are obliged to state that a reduction in the status of dance as an important medium of our culture is evident. What we are witnessing, as the role of dance in our times, is an impoverished remnant of its former great significance.

The disintegrated modern society has lost its direct contact with dance, and it is no longer an integral part of our group life. But, because of this, the necessity for children to participate directly in dance is greater than ever. For full development of all his potentialities, man needs to express himself through movement, using once again the primary medium of dance. This is desperately needed because it is a common biological urge. In this way, dance has the chance to be reintroduced into life again, into the life of the modern, urbanised, industrialised world. This was Rudolf Laban's idea, which is so often entirely misunderstood and distorted.

But to achieve this in our present-day civilisation we can no longer rely on intuition alone; intuition must be supported by our knowledge and understanding of all that dance means to man. Knowledge of facts ruling the development of dance makes it possible to interpret our contemporary needs. The area of scientifically-founded dance studies is badly needed. Unfortunately, choreology is only in its infancy.

The study of living dance forms in their own cultural context is the only way to acquire the knowledge of dance. Therefore there is the necessity to find places where dance is still a substantial element in human culture. This in turn often allows us to verify the written sources on dance. Thus it is mainly the "primitive" people's dance and dance folklore to which we have to turn. In this work, we are not just concerned with collecting "folk-dances," but we are also concerned with widening our knowledge of the essence of dance, of its nature. All the dances used by a human group will be of interest to us, even if we do not like them personally. The criterion of beauty is not essential in this type of investigation. This is perhaps the reason why Curt Sachs arrived at the following statement:

"... But here we come upon the question of the relationship between motor character and cultural development, any answer to which it must be the business of anthropology to give."[70]

REFERENCES

1. A. Lommel: *Prehistoric and Primitive Man*, p. 10.
2. K. Groos: *Die Spiele der Menschen*, p. 435.
   F. Boas: *The Function of Dance in Human Society*, p. 16.
   G. Buschan: *Neue Beiträge zur Menschen und Völkerkunde.*
3. J. A. M. Meerloo: *Dance Craze and Sacred Dance.*
4. R. Ohlmarks: *Studien zum Problem des Schamanismus.*
   M. Eliade: *Shamanism; Archaic Techniques of Ecstasy*, p. 449.
5. J. A. M. Meerloo: *Dance Craze and Sacred Dance*, p. 24.
6. *Ibid.*
7. L. E. Backman: *Religious Dances in the Christian Church and in Popular Medicine.*
8. E. Bourguignon: *Trance Dance*, p. 41.
9. A. W. Howitt: *The Native Tribes of South-east Australia*, p. 623.
10. E. Seler: *Fray Bernardino de Sahagun; Einige Kapitel aus seinem Geschichtswerk aus dem Aztekischen*, p. 231.
11. *Internationales Archiv für Ethnographie*, (1928), p. 161.
12. B. Stelmachowska: *"Podkoziolek" w obrzędach zapustnych Polski Zachodniej.*
13. J. S. Bystroń: *Zwyczaje żniwiarskie w Polsce.*
14. K. Moszyński: *Czlowiek*, pp. 152–53.
15. D. S. Janković: *Narodne igre*, Vol. IV, Part 2.
16. J. Kochanowski: *Pieśń świętojańska o Sobótce.*
17. D. S. Janković: *Narodne igre*, Vol. IV, Part 2.
18. *Ibid.*
19. D. S. and L. S. Janković: *Narodne igre*, Vol. V, Part 2.
20. D. S. and L. S. Janković: *Narodne igre*, Vol. IV, Part 2.
21. D. S. and L. S. Janković: *Narodne igre*, Vol. V, Part 2.
22. *Ibid.*
23. J. G. Frazer: *The Golden Bough*, p. 83.
24. *Ibid.*
25. R. Pösch: "Beobachtungen über Sprache, Gesänge und Tänze der Monumbo." In: *Mitteilungen der Anthropologischen Gesellschaft*, Wien, Vol. 35, (1905), p. 231.
26. K. Moszyński: *Kultura Ludowa Slowian*, Vol. II, Part 1, p. 273.

114   The Nature of Dance

27. F. Ratzel: *Völkerkunde*, Vol. II, p. 317.
28. D. S. and L. S. jankovic: *Narodne igre*, Vol. IV, Part 2.
29. J. S. Bystroń, *op. cit.*, p. 151.
30. *Ibid.*, p. 151.
31. *Ibid.*, p. 238.
32. O. Kolberg: *Lud, Poznańskie*, Vol. III, p. 153.
33. A. I. Hallowell: "Bear Ceremonialism in the Northern Hemisphere." In: *American Anthropologist*, XXVIII, (1926), pp. 1–175.
34. G. Kurath: "American Indian Dance in Ritual and Life." In: *The Folklorist*, Vol. VI, (1961–62), nos. 1 and 2.
35. B. Stelmachowska: *Rok Obrzędowy na Pomorzu*, p. 99.
36. G. Kurath: "American Indian Dance in Ritual and Life." In: *The Folklorist*, Vol. VII, (1961–62), no. 2, pp. 45–46.
37. W. C. Holden: *The Kaffir Races*, p. 192.
38. Mrs. French-Sheldon: "Customs among the Natives of East Africa." In: *Journal of the Anthropological Institute*, Vol. XXI, May (1892), pp. 366–67.
39. D. S. and L. S. Janković: *Narodne igre*, Vol. V, Part 2.
40. D. S. Janković: *Narodne igre*, Vol. IV, Part 2.
41. *Ibid.*
42. D. S. and L. S. Janković: *Narodne igre*, Vol. III, Chapter 4.
43. *Ibid.*
44. *Ibid.*
45. *Ibid.*
46. A. Oleszczuk: *Ludowe obrzędy weselne na Podlasiu*, p. 195.
47. W. Schram: *Ludowe obrzędy weselne we wsiach doliny Hoczewki i Tarnawki Ziemi Sanockiej*, p. 78.
48. A. Oleszczuk, *op. cit.*, p. 159.
49. St. Dworakowski: *Zwyczaje rodzinne w powiecie Wysoko-mazowieckim*, p. 87.
50. S. Benetowa: *Konopie w wierzeniach i zwyczajach ludowych*, p. 35.
51. B. Stelmachowska: *"Podkoziolek" w obrzędach zapustnych Polski Zachodniej*, p. 133.
52. A. Oleszczuk, *op. cit.*, p. 159.
53. D. S. and L. S. Janković: *Narodne igre*, Vol. V, Part 2.
54. L. and P. Bohannan: *Tiv of Central Nigeria*.
55. A. Fischer: *Zwyczaje pogrzebowe ludu polskiego*, p. 398.
56. M. Mead: *Growing up in New Guinea*, p. 133.
57. C. M. Bowra: *Primitive Song*, p. 9.
58. L. Lévy-Bruhl: *Les Fonctions mentales dans les Sociétés Inférieures*.
59. N. E. Miller and J. Dollard: *Social Learning and Imitation*.
    M. Mead, *op. cit.*, p. 38.
60. C. Baudouin de Courtenay Jędrzejewiczowa: "Folk Dances and Wedding Customs in Poland." In: *Archives de la Danse*, Paris, (1937).
61. C. Sachs: *World History of Dance*, pp. 47, 71, 80, 121, 125, 127.
62. C. Birket-Smith: *Geschichte der Kultur*, pp. 342–43.
63. R. H. Lowie: *Culture and Ethnology*, pp. 84–85.
64. W. Danckert: *Grundriss der Volksliedkunde*.
    F. Hoerburger: "On Relationships Between Music and Movement in Folk Dancing." In: *Journal I F M C*, Vol. XII, January (1960), p. 70.
65. P. Collaer and A. van der Linden: *Historical Atlas of Music*.
66. F. Boas: *The Function of Dance in Human Society*, p. 18.
67. E. E. Evans-Pritchard: "The Dance." In: *Africa*, Vol. I, no. 4, October (1928), p. 446.
68. A. B. Gomme: *The Traditional Games of England, Scotland, and Ireland*, p. xiv.
    K. Groos: *Die Spiele der Menschen*.
70. C. Sachs: *World History of Dance*, p. 34.

BIBLIOGRAPHY

ALFORD, V. *Sword Dance and Drama*, London: Merlin Press, 1962.
ANDERSSON, O. "The Revival of Folk Music and Folk Dancing in Finland," *Journal International Folk Music Council*, Vol. III, p. 6, Cambridge, 1951.
ANDRES, F. "Die Himmelreise der caräibischen Medizinmänner," *Zeitschrift für Ethnologie*, Vol. LXX, p. 3–5, Berlin, 1939.
APPUN, C. *Unter den Tropen*, Jena: Costenoble, 1871.
ARBEAU, T. *Orchesography*, trans. and ed. by C. W. Beaumont, London: 1925.
ARISTOTLE, *Poetics and Rhetoric*, London: J. M. Dent & Sons Ltd, 1953.
ARISTOXENUS, *Elements of Harmony*, ed. by P. Marquard, Berlin: 1868.
ARISTOXENUS, *Elements of Rhythm*, ed. by R. Westphal, Leipzig: 1861 and 1863.
ARMSTRONG, E. A. *Bird Display and Behaviour*, New York: Dover, 1965 (first publ. 1947).
ARNAUDOFF, M. *Die Bulgarischen Festbräuche*, Leipzig: 1912.
ATHENAEUS, *Deipnosophistai*, trans. by D. B. Gulick, London: Loeb Series, 1927–41.
Australia—Aboriginal Paintings—Arnhem Land, New York: Unesco World Art Series, 1954.
BAAREN, T. P. VAN, *Selbst die Götter tanzen; Sinn und Formen des Tanzes in Kultur und Religion*, Gütersloh: Verlagshaus G. Mohn, 1964.
BACKMAN, L. E. *Religious Dances in the Christian Church and in Popular Medicine*, trans. by E. Classen, London: Allen & Unwin, 1952.
BALOGH, J. "Tänze in Kirchen und auf Kirchhöfen," *Niederdeutsche Zeitschrift für Volkskunde*, Vol. 6, no. 1, p. 1–14, Hannover, 1928.
BARTENIEFF, I., DAVIS, M., and PAULAY, F. *Four Adaptations of Effort Theory in Research and Teaching*, New York: Dance Notation Bureau, 1970.
BAUDOUIN DE COURTENAY JĘDRZEJEWICZOWA, C. *Folk Dances and Wedding Customs in Poland*, Paris: Archives de la Danse, 1937.
BAYER, R. "The Essence of Rhythm," *Reflections on Art*, ed. by S. Langer, Oxford University Press, 1958 (first publ. 1953).
BECK, P. *Die Ecstase*, Sachsa: H. Haacke, 1906.
BENETOWA, S. *Konopie w wierzeniach i zwyczajach ludowych*, Warsaw: Prace etnologiczne TNW, 1936.
BENET, S. *Song, Dance, and Customs of Peasant Poland*, London: Dennis Dobson, 1951.

116   *The Nature of Dance*

BERGSON, H. *Essai sur les Données Immédiates de la Conscience*, Paris: F. Alcan, 1889.

BERGSON, H. *La Pensée et le Mouvant*, Paris: F. Alcan, 1934.

BERNE, E. *Games People Play; the Psychology of Human Relationships*, London: Penguin Books, 1968 (first publ. 1966).

BERTRAM, L. J. "The Origins of Drama," *Encyclopaedia Britannica*, Vol. VII, p. 628, Chicago: London, 1971.

BERTRAND, M. and DUMONT, M. *Expression Corporelle Mouvement et Pensée*, Paris: Libraire Philosophique, 1971.

BERTRAND, M. and DUMONT, M. *Les Bases Psycho-pédagogiques de l'Education Corporelle*, Paris: Libraire Philosophique, 1971.

BIRKET-SMITH, K. *Geschichte der Kultur; eine allgemeine Ethnologie*, München: Südwest Verlag, 1962 (first publ. 1941–42).

BLEEK, D., ROSENTHAL, E., GOODWIN, A. J. H. *Cave Artists of South Africa*, Cape Town: 1953.

BOAS, F. *Primitive Art*, New York: Dover Publications, 1955 (first publ. 1927).

BOAS, F. *The Function of Dance in Human Society*, New York: The Boas School, 1944.

BOEHN, M. VON, *Der Tanz*, Berlin: Wegweiser Verlag, 1925.

BOHANNAN, L. and P. "Tiv of Central Nigeria," *Ethnographic Survey of Africa: West Africa, Part VIII*. London: International African Institute, 1953.

BOURGUIGNON, E. *Trance Dance*, New York: Dance Perspectives no. 35, 1968.

BOWRA, C. M. *Primitive Song*, London: Weidenfeld & Nicolson, 1962.

BÖHME, F. "Massstäbe zu einer Geschichte der Tanzkunst", *Geist und Gesellschaft*, Vol. II, Breslau, 1927.

BREUIL, H. *Les Peintures Rupestres Schématiques de la Péninsule Ibérique*, Paris: Lagny, 1935.

BRINSON, P. *Background to European Ballet; A Collection of Studies relating to European Integration*, Leyden: A. W. Sijthoff, 1966.

BRODRICK, A. H. *Prehistoric Painting*, London: Avalon Press Ltd., 1948.

BROWN, F. A. JR. *Biological Clocks*, Boston: D. C. Heath, 1962.

BRÖMEL, C. H. *Fest-Täntze der ersten Christen und darauf erfolgte alte und neue Missbräuche bey den S. Johannis, Veitz, Elisabeths etc. Täntzen*, Jena: 1701.

BUBER, M. *Die Erzählungen der Hassidim*, Zürich: Manesse Verlag, 1949.

BURLAND, C. *Echoes of Magic; A Study of Seasonal Festivals through the Ages*, London: Peter Davies, 1972.

BUSCHAN, G. *Illustrierte Völkerkunde*, Berlin: 1922–23.

BUSCHAN, G. *Neue Beiträge zur Menschen- und Völkerkunde*, Dresden: C. Reissner, 1927.

BUSCHAN, G. *Die Sitten der Völker*, Stuttgart, Berlin and Leipzig: Union Deutsche Verlagsgesellschaft, 1914–1922.

BUYTENDIJK, F. J. J. *Wesen und Sinn des Spieles; Das Spielen des Menschen und der Tiere als Erscheinungsform der Lebenstriebe*, Berlin: K. Wolf, 1933.

BUYTENDIJK, F. J. J. "Das Spielerische und der Spieler," *Das Spiel*, Frankfurt/M., 1959.

BÜCHER, K. *Arbeit und Rhythmus*, Leipzig: B. G. Teubner, 1896.

BYSTROŃ, J. S. Zwyczaje żniwiarskie w Polsce, Cracow: A.U., 1916.

CAESARIUS, *Sermo 265. Dancing before the saints' churches*, Paris: Migne, 1865.

CAHUSAC, L. DE, *De la Danse Ancienne et Moderne*, Paris: La Haye, 1754.

CARMICHAEL, L. "Behaviour during Fetal Life", *Encyclopaedia of Psychology*, New York: Citadel Press, 1951.

CASSIRER, E. *An Essay on Man; An Introduction to a Philosophy of Human Culture*, New Haven: Yale University Press, 1944.

CHANCE, M. R. A. "The Nature and Special Features of the Instinctive Social Bond of Primates", *Social Life of Early Man*, ed. by S. L. Washburn, London: Methuen, 1962.

CHANCE, M., JOLLY, C. *Social Groups of Monkeys, Apes and Men*, London: Jonathan Cape, 1970.

CHARLES, L. HOERR, "Drama in Shaman Exorcism," *Journal of American Folklore*, Vol. LXVI, p. 95–122, Texas, April–June 1953.

CHILKOVSKY, N. "Techniques for the Choreologist," *Ethnomusicology*, Vol. V., p. 121–127, Wesleyan University Press, Middletown, Connecticut, 1961.

CICERO, *Speeches; Pro Murena*, London: The Loeb Series, W. Heinemann Ltd., 1937.

CLOUDSEY-THOMPSON, J. L. *Rhythmic Activity in Animal Physiology and Behaviour*, New York: Academic Press, 1961.

COGNIAT, R. *Danses d'Indochine*, Paris: Éditions des Chroniques du Jour, 1932.

COLLAER, P., VAN DER LINDEN, A. *Historical Atlas of Music*, London: George G. Harrap & Co. Ltd., 1968.

CORNFORD, F. M. *From Religion to Philosophy; A Study in the Origins of Western Speculations*, New York: Harper & Brothers, 1912, repr. 1957.

COURLANDER, H. *The Drum and the Hoe, Life and Lore of the Haitian People*, Berkeley and Los Angeles: University of California Press, 1960.

DAL, E. "The Faroese Folk-Song Chain Dance," *The Folklorist*, Vol. IV, no. 4, Manchester, 1957.

DANCKERT, W. *Grundriss der Volksliedkunde*, Berlin: B. Hahnefeld, 1939.

DANIÉLOU, A. *Bharata Nātyam*, Berlin: Institut für Vergleichende Musikstudien und Dokumentation, 1970.

DANIÉLOU, A., VATSYAYAN, K. *Kathakali*, Berlin: Institut für Vergleichende Musikstudien und Dokumentation, s.a.

DARWIN, C. *The Voyage of the "Beagle,"* London: J. Murray, 1845 (2nd ed.).

DARWIN, C. *The Expression of the Emotions in Man and Animals*, London: J. Murray, 1872.

DAVIDSON, D. S. "Aboriginal Australian and Tasmanian Rock Carvings and Paintings," *Memoirs of the American Philosophical Society*, Vol. V., Philadelphia, 1936.

DAWSON, C. *The Making of Europe; An Introduction to the History of European Unity*, London: Sheed and Ward, 1932.

DEAN-SMITH, M. "The Historical Progress of the English Social Dance," *The Proceedings of the Scottish Anthropological and Folklore Society*, Vol. IV, no. 1, Edinburgh, 1949.

DEAN-SMITH, M. "Folk-play origins of the English Masque," *Folk Lore*, Vol. LXV, London, Sept. 1954.

DELZA, S. "The Dance in the Chinese Theatre," *Journal of Aesthetics and Art Criticism*, Vol. XVI, no. 4, p. 437–52, New York, 1958.

DEMBOWSKI, J. *Psychologie der Affen*, transl. Berlin: 1956 (1st ed. Warsaw, 1946).

DETHIER, V. G., STELLAR, E. *Animal Behaviour*, New York: Prentice-Hall, 1970.

DEVI, R. *Dance Dialects of India*, Delhi and London: Vikas Publications, 1972.

DIDEROT, D. *Entretiens sur "Le Fils Naturel,"* (1757). Ed. F. C. Green, Cambridge: University Press, 1936.

DOMENICO DA PIACENZA, MS. first half of 15th century, Paris, Bibliothèque Nationale, Fonds It. no. 972.

DOUGLAS, M. *Purity and Danger; An Analysis of Concepts of Pollution and Taboo*, London: Routledge & Kegan Paul, 1966.

DOUGLAS, M. *Natural Symbols; Explorations in Cosmology*, London: Barrie & Rockliff, 1970 (2nd ed. 1973).

DWORAKOWSKI, S. *Zwyczaje rodzinne w powiecie Wysoko-mazowieckim*, Warsaw: TNW, 1935.

EDIRISINGHE, S. C. "Dance and Magic Drama in Ceylon," *Eastern Horizon*, Vol. I, no. 4, p. 47–49, Hong-Kong, 1960.

ELIADE, M. *Shamanism; Archaic Techniques of Ecstasy*, trans. W. R. Trask, London: Routledge & Kegan Paul Ltd., 1964 (1st ed. Paris, 1951).

ELIADE, M. *Patterns in Comparative Religion*, trans. R. Sheed, London: Sheed and Ward, 1958 (orig. ed. Paris, 1958).

ELIADE, M. *The Sacred and the Profane*, trans. W. R. Trask, New York: Harcourt, Brace & World Inc., 1959.

ELLIOTT, H. C. *The Shape of Intelligence; The Evolution of the Human Brain*, London: George Allen & Unwin, 1970.

ELLIS, H. *Studies in the Psychology of Sex*, London and Philadelphia: 1897–1928.

ELLIS, H. *The Dance of Life*, Boston and New York: Houghton Mifflin Company, 1923.

ELWIN, V. "The Hobby Horse and the Ecstatic Dance," *Folk Lore*, Vol. LIII, p. 209–13, London, Dec. 1942.

ENCYCLOPAEDIA BRITANNICA, 1st ed. (1768–71); 3rd ed. (1788–97); 9th ed. (1875–89); 10th ed. (1902–03); 14th ed. (1929, 1971).

EVANS-PRITCHARD, E. E. "The Dance," *Africa*, Vol. I, no. 4, p. 446–62, London, 1928.

EVANS-PRITCHARD, E. E. *Theories of Primitive Religion*, Oxford University Press, 1965.

FEATHERSTONE, C. *A Dialogue against light, lewde and lascivious dancing*, 1582, collection of the Bodleian Library, Oxford.

FERRERO, F. *The Art of Dancing, historically illustrated*, New York: 1859.

FIRTH, R. S. "Ritual and Drama in Malay Spirit Mediumship," *Comparative Studies in Society and History*, Vol. IX, p. 190–207, London, 1967.

FISCHER, A. *Zwyczaje pogrzebowe ludu polskiego*, Lwów: 1921.

FLETCHER, A. C. "Love Songs among the Omaha Indians," *Proceedings of the International Congress of Anthropology*, Chicago, 1893.

FOWLER, H. W. *A Dictionary of Modern English Usage*, Oxford University Press, 1966.

FOWLER, H. W. and F. G. *The Concise Oxford Dictionary*, Oxford University Press, 1969.

FOX, R. "The Cultural Animal," *Encounter*, London, July 1970.

FRAZER, J. G. *The Golden Bough: A Study in Magic and Religion*, London and Toronto: Macmillan & Co. Ltd., 1967 (first ed. 1890).

FRENCH-SHELDON, MRS. "Customs among the Natives of East Africa," *Journal of the Anthropological Institute*, Vol. XXI, p. 366–67, London, May 1892.

FRIEDRICH, A. "Knochen und Skelett in der Vorstellungswelt Nord-Asiens," *Wiener Beiträge zur Kulturgeschichte und Linguistik*, Vol. IV, Vienna, 1943.

FRISCH, K. VON, *The Dance Language and Orientation of Bees*, Oxford University Press, 1967 (orig. ed. Berlin, 1965).

FRITH, R. W. "Magic," *Encyclopaedia Britannica*, Vol. XIV, p. 572, Chicago and London, 1971.

FROBENIUS, L. *The Childhood of Man; A popular Account of the Lives,*

Customs, and Thoughts of Primitive Races, London: Seeley & Co, 1909.

FROBENIUS, L. and FOX, D. C. *Prehistoric Rock Pictures in Europe and Africa*, New York: Museum of Modern Art, 1937.

GALESKI, B. *Basic Concepts of Rural Sociology*, trans. H. C. Stevens, Manchester University Press, 1972.

GAUTIER, T. *Histoire de l'Art Dramatique en France depuis Vingt-cinq Ans*, Brussels: Edition Hetzel, 1858–59.

GAUTIER, T. *The Romantic Ballet as seen by Théophile Gautier*, trans. by C. Beaumont, London: 1932.

GEORGIADES, T. *Der Griechische Rhythmus; Musik, Reigen, Vers und Sprache*, Hamburg: 1949.

GEORGIADES, T. *Musik und Rhythmus bei den Griechen; Zum Ursprung der abendländischen Musik*, Hamburg: Rowohlt, 1958.

GIEDION, S. *The Eternal Present; The Beginnings of Art*, Oxford University Press, 1962.

GODLEWSKI, A. L. *Kultury zbieracze i łowieckie*, Warsaw: University Script, 1950.

GOETSCH, W. *Vergleichende Biologie der Insekten-Staaten*, Leipzig: Becker & Erler, 1940.

GOMBRICH, E. H. *The Story of Art*, London and New York: Phaidon Publ., 1950.

GOMME, A. B. *The Traditional Games of England, Scotland, and Ireland—with Tunes, Singing-rhymes, and Methods of Playing according to the Variants extant and recorded in different Parts of the Kingdom*, London: 1894–1898.

GOUGAUD, L. "La Danse dans les Églises," *Revue d'histoire ecclésiastique*, Vol. XV, no. 5, p. 229, Paris, 1914.

GRAF, W. "Die Tanzschrift als wissenschaftliches Hilfsmittel," *Mitteilungen der Anthropologischen Gesellschaft*, Vol. LXXXIV– LXXXV, p. 83–91, Vienna, 1955.

GRAZIOSI, P. *Palaeolithic Art*, London: Faber & Faber, 1960.

GREGOR, J. *Kulturgeschichte des Balletts*, Vienna: Gallus Verlag, 1944.

GROOS, K. *Die Spiele der Tiere*, Jena: Gustav Fischer Verlag, 1896.

GROOS, K. *Die Spiele der Menschen*, Jena: Gustav Fischer Verlag, 1899.

GROSLIER, G. *Danseuses Cambodgiennes*, Paris: Augustin Challamel, 1913.

GROSSE, E. *Die Anfänge der Kunst*, Freiburg: J. C. B. Mohr, 1894.

GUEST, I. *The Romantic Ballet in England*, London: Pitman Publ., 1954.

GUEST, I. *A Gallery of Romantic Ballet; A Catalogue of the Collection of Prints at the Mercury Theatre*, London: New Mercury Ltd, 1965.

GUEST, I. *The Romantic Ballet in Paris*, London: Sir Isaac Pitman and Sons Ltd., 1966.

GUILCHER, J. M. *La Tradition populaire de danse en Basse-Bretagne*, Paris: Mouton & Co., 1963.

GUILCHER, J. M. "Aspects et problèmes de la danse populaire traditionnelle," *Ethnologie française*, Vol. I, no. 2, p. 7, Paris, 1971.

GUNDA, B. "Die mitteleuropäischen Bauernkulturen und die Methode der 'Cultural Anthropology'," *VIe Congrès International des Sciences Anthropologiques et Ethnologiques, Paris, 1960*, Vol. II, no. 1, p. 543, Musée de l'Homme, Paris, 1963.

GUNJI, M. *Buyo; The Classical Dance*, New York and Kyoto: Weatherhill, 1970.

GUSINDE, M. *Die Feuerland Indianer; Ergebnisse meiner vier Forschungsreisen in den Jahren 1918 bis 1924 unternommen im Auftrage des Ministerio de Instrucción Pública de Chile*, Mödling bei Vienna: Anthropos, 1931.

HAGEMANN, C. *Spiele der Völker; Eindrücke und Studien auf einer Weltfahrt nach Africa und Ost-Asien*, Berlin: Schuster und Loeffler, 1919.

HAKANSSON, T. "Sex in Primitive Art and Dance," *Encyclopaedia of Sexual Behaviour*, p. 154–60, New York: Hawthorn Books Inc., 1961.

HALL, E. T. *The Silent Language*, New York: Doubleday & Co. Inc., 1959.

HALL, G. S. *Adolescence; its Psychology and its Relations to Physiology, Anthropology, Sociology, Sex, Crime, Religion and Education*, New York: D. Appleton & Co., 1904.

HALLOWELL, A. I. "Bear Ceremonialism in the Northern Hemisphere," *American Anthropologist*, Vol. XXVIII, Menasha, 1926.

HALLOWELL, A. I. "Self, Society and Culture in Phylogenetic Perspective," *Evolution after Darwin*, Vol. II, p. 309–371, Chicago University Press, 1960.

HAMBLY, W. D. *Tribal Dancing and Social Development*, London: Witherby, 1926.

HARPER, P. *Studies in Nigerian Dance. No. 1; Tiv Women. The Icough Dance*, (film comment), Institute of African Studies, University of Ibadan, 1966.

HARPER, P. *Studies in Nigerian Dance. No. 2; The Miango Dancers. The Irigwe Dancers of Miango Village on the Jos Plateau*, (film comment), Institute of African Studies, University of Ibadan, 1966.

HARPER, P. "Dance Studies," *African Notes*, Vol. IV, no. 3, Institute of African Studies, University of Ibadan, May 1968.

122 *The Nature of Dance*

HARRISON, J. E. *Ancient Art and Ritual*, Oxford University Press, 1913.

HELMS-BLASCHE, A. *Bunte Tänze wie wir sie suchten und fanden*, Leipzig: Friedrich Hofmeister, 1957.

HENNEY, J. *Trance Behaviour among Shakers of St. Vincent*, Working Paper No. 8, Cross-Cultural Studies of Disassociational States, Columbus: The Ohio State University, 1967.

HEUSLER, A. "Deutsche Versgeschichte," *Grundriss der Germanischen Philologie*, Vol. VIII, p. 17, Berlin, 1925.

HEWES, G. W. "Primate Communication and the Gestural Origin of Language," *Current Anthropology*, Vol. 14, no. 1–2, p. 5–24, Chicago, Feb.–April 1973.

HOERBURGER, F. "Dance Notation and Folk Dance Research," *Journal International Folk Music Council*, Vol. X, p. 62, Cambridge, 1958.

HOERBURGER, F. "Study of Folk Dance and the need for a uniform Method of Dance Notation," *Journal International Folk Music Council*, Vol. XI, p. 71–3, Amsterdam, 1959.

HOERBURGER, F. "Sinn und Weg der Volkstanzkunde," *Kontakte*, p. 132, Mainz, 1959.

HOERBURGER, F. "On Relationships between Music and Movement in Folk Dancing," *Journal International Folk Music Council*, Vol. XII, p. 70, Amsterdam, 1960.

HOLDEN, W. C. *The Past and Future of the Kaffir Races*, London: 1866.

HOPKINS, L. C. "The Shaman or Chinese Wu; His Inspired Dancing and Versatile Charakter," *Journal of the Royal Asiatic Society*, p. 3–16, London, 1945.

HOWITT, A. W. *The Native Tribes of South-east Australia*, London: Macmillan & Co., 1904.

HUIZINGA, J. *The Waning of the Middle Ages*, Harmondsworth: Penguin Books, 1955 (first publ. 1919).

HUIZINGA, J. *Homo Ludens*, London: Routledge & Kegan Paul Ltd., 1949 (first publ. 1938).

HUTCHINSON, A. *Labanotation; The System for Recording Movement*, London: Phoenix House Ltd., 1954.

HYE-KERKDAL, K. H. "Tanz als Akkulturationsproblem," *Tribus*, Vol. IX, p. 164–71, Stuttgart, 1960.

ILIJIN, M. "Influences réciproques des danses urbaines et traditionnelles en Yougoslavie," *Studia Musicologica A. Sc. Hungaricae*, Vol. VII, no. 1–4, Budapest, 1965.

JAMES, E. O. "Prehistoric Religion," *Man and his Gods*, London and New York: Hamlyn, 1971.

JANKOVIĆ, D. S. and L. S. *Narodne Igre*, Belgrade: 1934–64.

JANCOVIĆ, L. S. and D. S. "Dancing without a Musical Accompaniment

... In Yugoslavia," *The Folklorist*, Vol. V, no. 4, p. 263–65, Manchester, 1959.

JEANMAIRE, H. *Dionysos; Histoire du Culte de Bacchus*, Paris: Payot, 1951.

JELINKOVÁ, Z. *Točivé tance*, Gottwaldov: Krajské nakladatelstvi, 1959.

JELINKOVÁ, Z. "Drehtänze," *Journal International Folk Music Council*, Vol. XV, p. 167, Cambridge, 1963.

JUNG, C. G. *Man and His Symbols*, London: Aldus Books, 1964.

JUNK, V. *Handbuch des Tanzes*, Stuttgart: E. Klett, 1930.

KADMAN, G. "Yemenite Dances and their Influence on the new Israeli Folk Dances," *Journal International Folk Music Council*, Vol. IV, p. 27, Cambridge, 1952.

KAEPPLER, A. L. "Acculturation in Hawaiian Dance," *Yearbook International Folk Music Council*, Vol. IV, p. 38–46, Kingston, 1972.

KAEPPLER, A. L. "Method and Theory in Analyzing Dance Structure with an Analysis of Tongan Dance," *Ethnomusicology*, Vol. XVI, no. 2, p. 173–217, New Orleans, May 1972.

KAINZ, F. *Die "Sprache" der Tiere*, Stuttgart: Enke, 1961.

KALVODOVÁ-SÍS-VANIŠ, *Chinese Theatre*, London: Spring Books, s.a.

KARPELES, M. *Cecil Sharp; His Life and Work*, London: Routledge and Kegan Paul, 1967.

KARTOMI, M. J. "Music and Trance in Central Java," *Ethnomusicology*, Vol. XVII, no. 2, p. 163–208, Austin, Texas, May 1973.

KELSEN, H. *Society and Nature; A Sociological Inquiry*, Chicago University Press, 1943.

KEMP, P. *Healing Ritual; Studies in the technique and Tradition of the Southern Slavs*. London: Faber and Faber, 1928.

KENNEDY, D. "Dramatic Elements in the Folk Dance," *Journal English Folk Dance and Song Society*, Vol. VI, no. 1, London, 1949.

KENNEDY, D. *England's Dances; Folk Dancing To-day and Yesterday*, London: G. Bell and Sons, Ltd., 1949.

KENNEDY, D. "The English Morris Dance and its European Analogues," *The Proceedings of the Scottish Anthropological and Folklore Society*, Vol. IV, no. 1, Edinburgh, 1949.

KENNEDY, D. "England's Ritual Dances," *Journal International Folk Music Council*, Vol. II, p. 8, Cambridge, 1950.

KEPES, G. *The Nature and Art of Motion*, London: Studio Vista, 1965.

KNUST, A. *Abriss der Kinetographie Laban*, Hamburg: Das Tanzarchiv, 1956. Engl. version: *Handbook of Kinetography Laban*, Hamburg: Das Tanzarchiv, 1958.

KNUST, A. "The Notation of Details in National Dances," *Dance Notation Record*, Vol. XI, no. 2, p. 2–3, New York, 1960.

KOCHANOWSKI, J. *Pieśń świętojańska o Sobótce*, Cracow: Drukarnia Lazarzowa, 1586.

KOLBERG, O. *Lud*, Warsaw and Cracow: 1857–1910.

KOOL, J. *Tänze der Naturvölker; ein Deutungsversuch primitiver Tanzkulte und Kultgebräuche*, Berlin: A. Fürstner, 1921.

KOWALEWSKY, M. "Marriage among the Early Slavs," *Folk Lore*, Vol. I, p. 463, London, 1890.

KÖHLER, W. "Nachweis einfacher Strukturfunktionen beim Schimpanzen und beim Haushuhn," *Abhandlungen Preussischer Akademie der Wissenschaften*, Berlin, 1915.

KÖHLER, W. *Intelligenzprüfungen an Menschenaffen*, Berlin: J. Springer, 1921.

KRIER, J. B. *Die Springprozession und die Wahlfahrt zum Grabe des heiligen Willibrord in Echternach*, Luxembourg: 1871.

KUMMER, H. *Primate Societies; Group Techniques of Ecological Adaptation*, Chicago: Aldine Atherton, 1970.

KUNST, J. *Metre, Rhythm, Multipart Music*, Leiden: E. J. Brill, 1950.

KURATH, G. P. "Choreology and Anthropology," *American Anthropologist*, Vol. LVIII, no. 1, p. 177–79, Menasha, 1956.

KURATH, G. P. "Panorama of Dance Ethnology," *Current Anthropology*, Vol. I, no. 3, p. 233–54, Chicago, 1960.

KURATH, G. P. "American Indian Dance in Ritual and Life," *The Folklorist*, Vol. VI and VII, Manchester, 1961–62.

KURATH, G. P., MARTI, S. *Dances of Anáhuac; The Choreography and Music of Precortesian Dances*, New York: Wenner-Gren Foundation for Anthropological Research, Inc., 1964.

KURATH, G. P. "Native Choreographic Areas of North America," *American Anthropologist*, Vol. LV, no. 1, p. 60–73, Menasha, 1953.

KÜHN, H. *The Rock Pictures of Europe*, London: Sidgwick & Jackson & McGraw, 1956 (first publ. 1952).

LABAN, R. *Die Welt des Tänzers*, Stuttgart: W. Seifert, 1920.

LABAN, R. *Choreographie*, Jena: E. Diederichs, 1926.

LABAN, R. "La Danse dans l'Opera," *Archives inter. de la danse*, no. 1, p. 10–11, Paris, 1933.

LABAN, R., LAWRENCE, F. C. *Effort*, London: Macdonald & Evans Ltd., 1947.

LABAN, R. *Modern Educational Dance*, London: Macdonald & Evans Ltd., 1948.

LABAN, R. *The Mastery of Movement*, London: Macdonald & Evans Ltd., 1960.

LABAN, R. *Principles of Dance and Movement Notation*, London: Macdonald & Evans Ltd., 1956.

LABAN, R. *Rudolf Laban speaks about Movement and Dance*, Addlestone: The Laban Art of Movement Centre, 1971.

LA BARRE, W. *The Human Animal*, Chicago University Press, 1954.

LA BARRE, W. *The Ghost Dance; The Origins of Religion*, London: Allen & Unwin Ltd., 1972 (first publ. 1970).

LAJOUX, J. D. *Rock Paintings of Tassili*, London and Bergamo: Thames & Hudson, 1963.

LAMB, W. *Posture and Gesture; An Introduction to the Study of Physical Behaviour*, London: Gerald Duckworth & Co. Ltd., 1965.

LAMB, W., TURNER, D. *Management Behaviour*, London: Gerald Duckworth & Co. Ltd., 1969.

LANGE, R. *Taniec ludowy w pracach Muzeum Etnograficznego w Toruniu; Metoda pracy i kwestionariusz*, Toruń: Muzeum Etnograficzne, 1960.

LANGE, R. "Tańce kujawskie," *Literatura Ludowa*, no. 4, p. 13–20, Warsaw, 1964.

LANGE, R. "Der Volkstanz in Polen," *Deutsches Jahrbuch für Volkskunde*, Vol. XII, part 2, p. 342–357, Berlin, 1966.

LANGE, R. "Kinetography Laban (Movement Notation) and the Folk Dance Research in Poland," *Lud*, Vol. L, p. 378–91, Wrocław, 1966.

LANGE, R. "The Traditional Dances of Poland," *Viltis*, Vol. XXIX, no. 1, p. 4–14, Denver, 1970.

LANGE, R. "The Nature of Dance," *Laban Art of Movement Guild Magazine*, May, 1970.

LANGE, R. "Every Man a Dancer," *Anniversary Issue—Laban Art of Movement Studio*, Addlestone, 1971.

LANGER, S. *Philosophy in a New Key; A Study in the Symbolism of Reason, Rite and Art*, Cambridge Mass.: Harvard University Press, 1942.

LANGER, S. *Feeling and Form: A Theory of Art*, London: Routledge & Kegan Paul Ltd., 1953.

LANGER, S. *Problems of Art; Ten Philosophical Lectures*, London: Routledge & Kegan Paul Ltd., 1957.

LA SORSA, S. "Song and Dance in Puglia and Lucania," *Ricreazione*, Vol. I, no. 7–8, Rome, 1949.

LAWLER, L. B. *The Dance in Ancient Greece*, London: Adam & Charles Black, 1964.

LEEUW, G. VAN DER, *Wegen en Grenzen*, Amsterdam: H. J. Paris, 1948.

LEEUW, G. VAN DER, *Sacred and Profane Beauty: The Holy in Art*, trans. D. E. Green, Nashville and New York: Abingdon Press, 1963.

LEIRIS, M. *La Possession et ses aspects théâtraux chez les Ethiopiens de Gondar*, Paris: Plon, 1958.

LELYVELD. T. B. VAN, *La Danse dans le Théâtre Javanais*, Paris: Libr. Floury, 1931.

126   *The Nature of Dance*

LENNEBERG, E. H. *Biological Foundations of Language*, New York: John Wiley & Sons, 1967.

LENOIS, R. "La danse comme institution sociale," *Anthropologie*, Vol. IL, p. 411–29, Paris, 1931.

LÉVI-STRAUSS, C. *Totemism*, Harmondsworth: Penguin Books Ltd., 1969 (first publ. 1962).

LÉVI-STRAUSS, C. *Structural Anthropology*, London: Penguin Press, 1968 (first publ. 1958).

LEVINSON, A. "The Idea of the Dance from Aristotle to Mallarmé," *Theatre Arts Monthly*, Vol. IX, no. 8, p. 571–83, New York, 1927.

LÉVY-BRUHL, L. *Les Fonctions mentales dans les Sociétés Inférieures*, Paris: Bibliothèque de Philosophie contemporaine, 1910.

LIEBERMANN, F. "Englische Vergnügungen auf Kirchhöfen," *Archiv für das Studium der neueren Sprachen und Litteratur*, Vol. 65, p. 180, Braunschweig, 1911.

LIBERMANN, F. "Liturgical Dances," *The Sacristy*, Vol. I, p. 63, London, 1871.

LOMAX, A. *Folk Song Style and Culture*, Washington: American Association for the Advancement of Science, 1968.

LOMAX, A. "Cantometrics—Choreometrics Projects," *Yearbook International Folk Music Council*, p. 142–45, Kingston, 1972.

LOMMEL, A. *The World of the Early Hunters*, London: Cory, Adams and Mackay, and McGraw-Hill, 1966.

LOMMEL, A. *Prehistoric and Primitive Man*, London: Paul Hamlyn, 1966.

LOMMEL, A. "Der Schamanismus," *Naturvölker in unserer Zeit*, Stuttgart: Deutsche Verlags-Anstalt, 1971.

LORENZ, K. *On Aggression*, London: Methuen & Co. Ltd., 1967 (first publ. 1963).

LORENZ, K. *Studies in Animal and Human Behaviour*, London: Methuen & Co. Ltd. 1970.

LORENZEN, P. "The Revival of Folk Dancing in Denmark," *Journal International Folk Music Council*, Vol. I, p. 24, Cambridge, 1949.

LOUIS, M. L. A. "Les origines préhistoriques de la danse," *Cahiers de Préhistoire d'Archéologie*, Vol. IV, p. 3–37, Montpellier, 1955.

LOUIS, M. A. L. *Le Folklore et la Danse*, Paris: G.P. Maisonneuve et Larose, 1963.

LOWIE, R. H. *Culture and Ethnology*, New York and London: Basic Books, Inc. 1966, (first publ. 1917).

LOWIE, R. H. *An Introduction to Cultural Anthropology*, New York: Farrar & Rinehart, 1934.

LOZOYA, MARQUES DE, *Historia del Arte Hispanico*, Barcelona: Salvat, 1931.

LUCIAN, *Lucian of Samosata from the Greek with the comments of*

Wieland and others, by William Tooke, F.R.S., London: Longman, Hurst, Rees, Orme & Brown, 1820.

LÜBECK, K. L. "Die Krankheitsdämonen der Balkanvölker," *Zeitschrift des Vereins für Volkskunde*, Vol. IX, p. 295, Berlin, 1899.

MACLAREN, J. *My Crowded Solitude*, New York: R. M. McBride & Co., 1926.

MALINOWSKI, B. *The Sexual Life of Savages in North Western Melanesia*, London: G. Routledge & Sons, 1929.

MALINOWSKI, B. "Magic, Science and Religion," *Science, Religion, and Reality*, ed. by J. Needham, London: Sheldon Press, 1925.

MALINOWSKI, B. *Coral Gardens and their Magic*, London: G. Allen & Unwin, 1935.

MARECHAL, S. *Danses Cambodgiennes*, Saigon: Editions de la Revue Extrême Asie, 1926.

MARETT, R. R. *The Threshold of Religion*, London: Methuen & Co., 1914 (first publ. 1909).

MAROLT, F., ŠUŠTAR, M. *Slovenski Ljudski Plesi—Koroške*, Ljubljana: Glasbeno Narodopisni Institut, 1958.

MARRINGER, J. *L'homme préhistorique et ses dieux*, Paris: Ed. Arthaud, 1958.

MARSHALL, L. "The Kung Bushmen of the Kalahari Desert," *Peoples of Africa*, ed. J. L. Gibbs, London: 1965.

MARTIN, A. "Geschichte der Tanzkrankheit in Deutschland," *Zeitschrift des Vereins für Volkskunde*, Vol. XXIV, p. 113–34, 225–39, Berlin, 1914.

MARTIN, A. "Die Tanzkrankheit in der Schweiz," *Medizinische Wochenschrift*, Vol. IV, p. 470, Hamburg, 1923.

MARTIN, G., PESOVAR, E. "A Structural Analysis of the Hungarian Folk Dance," *Acta Ethnographica*, Vol. X, no. 1–2, p. 1–40, Budapest, 1961.

MARTIN, G., PESOVAR, E. "Determination of Motive Types in Dance Folklore," *Acta Ethnographica*, Vol. XII, no. 3–4, p. 295–331, Budapest, 1963.

MARTIN, G. "Considérations sur l'analyse des relations entre la danse et la musique de danse populaires," *Studia Musicologica*, Vol. VII, no. 1–4, p. 315–338, Budapest, 1965.

MARTIN, G. "Dance Types in Ethiopia," *Journal International Folk Music Council*, Vol. XIX, p. 23, Cambridge, 1967.

MARTINO, E. DE, *La Terra del Rimorso*, Milan: 1961.

MEAD, M. *Growing up in New Guinea*, Harmondsworth: Penguin Books Ltd., 1968 (first publ. 1930).

MEERLOO, J. A. M. *Communication and Conversation*, New York: International Universities Press, 1952.

MEERLOO, J. A. M. "Archaic Behaviour and the Communicative

Act," *Psychiatric Quarterly*, Vol. XXIX, p. 60–73, New York, 1955.

MEERLOO, J. A. M. *Dance Craze and Sacred Dance*, London: Peter Owen, 1962 (first publ. 1961).

MEERLOO, J. A. M. "Dancing for the right or wrong Reasons," *Anthology of Impulse*, ed. M. van Tuyl, New York: Dance Horizons, 1969.

MENDOZA, V. T. "Folk Origins of the Mexican Tango," *Nuestra Música*, no. 18, Mexico, 1950.

MENESTRIER, C.-F. *Des Ballets Anciens et Modernes selon les Règles du Théâtre*, Genève: Minkoff Reprint, 1972 (first publ. 1682).

MESSING, S. D. "Group therapy and social status in the zar cult of Ethiopia," *American Anthropologist*, Vol. LX, p. 1120–26, Menasha, 1958.

MILLAR, S. *The Psychology of Play*, London: Penguin Books, 1968.

MILLER, N. E., DOLLARD, J. *Social Learning and Imitation*, New Haven and London: Yale University Press, 1941.

MINKOWSKI, M. "Neurobiologische Studien am Menschlichen Fötus," *Handbuch Biologischer Arbeitsmethoden*, Vol. V, 1928.

MOGGRIDGE, J. T. *Harvesting Ants and Trap-Door Spiders*, London: L. Reeve & Co., 1873.

MONTAGU, A. ed. *Man and Aggression*, New York: Galaxy Books OUP, 2nd ed. 1974.

MOONEY, J. "The Ghost Dance Religion and the Sioux Outbreak of 1890," *14th Annual Report, Bureau of American Ethnology*, part 2, p. 641–1136, Washington, 1896.

MOSZYŃSKI, K. *Kultura Ludowa Słowian*, Cracow, 1929–34–39.

MOSZYŃSKI, K. *Człowiek; Wstęp do etnografii powszechnej i etnologii*, Wrocław: Ossolineum, 1958.

MOUNTFORD, C. P. *Aboriginal Paintings from Australia*, London: Fontana Unesco Art Books, 1964.

MOURA, J. *Le Royaume du Cambodge*, Paris: Leroux, 1883.

MÜNSTERBERG, H. "Society and the Dance," *Psychology and Social Sanity*, p. 273–88, New York: Doubleday, 1914.

NAIDU, B. V. NARAYANASWAMI; NAIDU, P. SRINIVASULU; PANTULU, O. V. RANGAYYA, *Tāndava Laksanam or the Fundamentals of Ancient Hindu Dancing*, New Delhi: Munshiram Manoharlal, 1936.

NAKAMURA, Y. *Noh; The Classical Theater*, New York & Tokyo: Weatherhill, 1971.

NASELLI, C. "Aspects de la danse rituelle en Italie," *Journal International Folk Music Council*, Vol. VI, p. 15–17, New York, 1954.

NEOG, M. "Three Dance Styles of Assam," *Journal of the Music Academy*, Vol. XXXI, p. 138–145, Madras, 1960.

NETTL, B. *Music in Primitive Culture*, Cambridge: Harvard University Press, 1956.

NETTL, P. *The Story of Dance Music*, New York: Philosophical Library, 1947.

NEWELL, W. W. *Games and Songs of American Children*, New York: Dover, 1963 (first publ. 1883).

NKETIA, J. H. "Possession Dances in African Societies," *Journal International Folk Music Council*, Vol. IX, p. 4–8, Cambridge, 1957.

NKETIA KWABENA, J. H. "The Interrelations of African Music and Dance," *Studia Musicologica*, Vol. VII, no. 1–4, p. 91–101, Budapest, 1965.

NORTH, M. *Personality Assessment through Movement*, London: Macdonald & Evans Ltd. 1972.

NOVERRE, J. G. *Letters on Dancing and Ballets*, trans. C. W. Beaumont, London: C. W. Beaumont, 1930. (orig. publ. 1760).

NOYEN, A. "De l'Origine et du But véritable de la Procession dansante d'Echternach," *Bull. de l'Inst. archéol. Liégeois*, Vol. XV, p. 223, Liége, 1880.

OESTERLEY, W. O. E. *The Sacred Dance*, Cambridge: University Press, 1923.

OHLMARKS, R. *Studien zum Problem des Schamanismus*, Lund: 1939.

OLESZCZUK, A. *Ludowe obrzędy weselne na Podlasiu*, Lublin and Lódź: PTL, 1951.

OMIBIYI, M. "Folk Music and Dance in African Education," *Yearbook International Folk Music Council*, Vol. IV, p. 87–94, Kingston, 1972.

ONIONS, C. T. *The Oxford Dictionary of English Etymology*, Oxford University Press, 1967.

OPIE, I. and P. *Children's Games in Street and Playground*, Oxford University Press, 1969.

OTTO, W. F. *Menschengestalt und Tanz*, Munich: 1956.

PAJTONDŽIEV, G. *Makedonski Narodni Ora*, Skopje: Makedonska Kniga, 1973.

PARRINDER, G. *Man and his Gods*, London: Hamlyn, 1971.

PENNA, R. *La Tarantella Napoletana; Storia e Leggende*, Naples: Rivista di Etnografia, 1963.

PESCHEL, O. *Völkerkunde*, Leipzig: Altenburg, 1874.

PESOVÁR, E. "Der heutige Stand der ungarischen Volkstanzforschung," *Journal International Folk Music Council*, Vol. XV, p. 53–57, Cambridge, 1963.

PESOVÁR, E. "Les types de la danse folklorique hongroise," *Studia Musicologica*, Vol. VII, Fasc. 1–4, Budapest, 1965.

PETERMANN, K. *Syllabus der Volkstanzanalyse*, Leipzig: IFMC, 1965.

PETRI, H. "Traum und Trance bei den Australoiden," *Naturvölker in unserer Zeit*, Stuttgart: Deutsche Verlags-Anstalt, 1971.

PIAGET, J. *The Child's Conception of Time*, London: Routledge & Kegan Paul, 1969 (orig. publ. 1927).

PIAGET, J. *The Child's Conception of Movement and Speed*, London: Routledge & Kegan Paul, 1970 (orig. publ. 1946).

PIAGET, J., INHELDER, B. *The Child's Conception of Space*, London: Routledge & Kegan Paul, 1956 (orig. publ. 1948).

PIAGET, J. *The Origin of Intelligence in the Child*, London: Routledge & Kegan Paul, 1956 (orig. publ. 1948).

PIASECKI, E. "Tradycyjne gry i zabawy ruchowe oraz ich geneza," *40 lat od Katedry Wychowania Fizycznego UP do WSWF w Poznaniu*, Poznań: WSWF, 1959.

PINON, R. "La danse folklorique en Wallonie; problèmes et conditions de sa revitalisation," *Fédération Wallonne des groupements de danses populaires—Feuillets d'Information*, no. 13, Brussels, 1962.

PIPREK, J. "Slavische Brautwerbungs- und Hochzeitsgebräuche," *Zeitschrift für österreichische Volkskunde*, Vol. XIX, (add. Vol. IX), Stuttgart, 1914.

PLATO, *Laws*, trans. by R. G. Bury, London: W. Heinemann, 1952.

PLESSEN, V. VON, "Bei den Flussvölkern von Borneo," *Atlantis*, Vol. VIII, Berlin, 1936.

PLICKA, K. "Slovakische Kinderspiele," *Journal International Folk Music Council*, Vol. XV, p. 168, Cambridge, 1963.

POOVIAH, S. "Art and Science of Indian Classical Dance and its Social Bearing," *Journal of the University of Bombay*, Vol. XX, Bombay, 1951.

PÖSCH, R. "Beobachtungen über Sprache, Gesänge und Tänze der Monumbo," *Mitteilungen der Anthropologischen Gesellschaft*, Vol. 35, Vienna, 1905.

PRESTON, V. *A Handbook for Modern Educational Dance*, London: Macdonald & Evans Ltd., 1963.

PRESTON-DUNLOP, V. *Practical Kinetography Laban*, London: Macdonald & Evans Ltd., 1969.

PREUSS, K. T. "Ursprung der Religion und Kunst," *Globus*, Vol. LXXXVI, Braunschweig, 1904.

PRIDDIN, D. *The Art of the Dance in French Literature*, London: Adam and Charles Black, 1952.

PROCA-CIORTEA, P. "On Rhythm in Rumanian Folk Dance," *Yearbook International Folk Music Council*, Vol. I, p. 176–199, Urbana, 1969.

QUASTEN, J. "Musik und Gesang in den Kulten der heidnischen Antike und christlichen Frühzeit," *Liturgiegeschichtlichen Quellen und Forschungen*, Vol. XXV, Münster, 1930.

RADIN, P. *The Method and Theory of Ethnology; An Essay in Criticism*, New York and London: McGraw-Hill Book Co., Inc. 1933.

RAFFLES, T. S. *The History of Java*, London: Black, Parburg and Allen, 1817.

RAMANATHAN, S. B. S. "A Survey of the Traditions of Music, Dance and Drama in the Madras State," *Bulletin of the Institute of Traditional Cultures*, Vol. II, p. 214–221, Madras, 1960.

RAMEAU, P. *The Dancing Master*, trans. C. W. Beaumont, London: C. W. Beaumont, 1931 (orig. publ. 1725).

RAMSDEN, P. *Top Team Planning; A Study of the Power of Individual Motivation in Management*, London: Cassell, Associated Business Programmes Ltd., 1973.

RATZEL, F. *Völkerkunde*, Leipzig: Bibliographisches Institut, 1885–88.

RAWLINGS, M. K. *The Yearling*, New York: Scribner's, 1938.

READ, H. *Art and Society*, London: Faber and Faber, 1967 (first publ. 1936).

READ, H. "The Biological Significance of Art," *Saturday Evening Post*, 26th Sept., Philadelphia, 1959.

READ, H. *The origin of Form in Art*, London: Thames and Hudson, 1965.

REHNSBERG, M. *Swedish Folk Dances*, Stockholm: Nordiska Museum and Skansen, 1939.

REID, L. A. *Meaning in the Arts*, London: Allen and Unwin, 1969.

REIMERS, A. "Die Springprozession zu Echternach," *Frankfurter Zeitgennossischen Broschüren*, Vol. V, p. 240, Frankfurt, 1884.

RENSCH, B. "The Laws of Evolution," *Evolution after Darwin*, Vol. I, p. 95–116, Chicago: University Press, 1960.

RIDGEWAY, W. *The Dramas and Dramatic Dances of the Non-European Races*, Cambridge University Press, 1915.

RIEMANN, H. *Musikalische Dynamik und Agogik*, Hamburg: Rahter, 1884.

RITTER, H. "Der Reigen der tanzenden Derwische," *Zeitschrift für Vergleichende Musikwissenschaft*, Vol. I, no. 2, p. 28–40, 1933.

ROBB, J. D. "Matachines Dance, a ritual Folk Dance," *Western Folklore*, Vol. XX, no. 2, p. 87–101, Berkeley, 1961.

ROBINS, F. and J. *Educational Rhythmics for Mentally Handicapped Children; A Method of Practical Application*, Rapperswil: Ra-Verlag, 1963.

ROUHIER, A. *La plante qui fait les yeux émerveillés*, Paris: G. Doin, 1927.

ROSA Y LÓPEZ, DON SIMON DE LA, *Los Seises de la Catedral de Sevilla*, Sevilla: 1904.

ROSEN, E. *Dance in Psychotherapy*, New York: Teachers College, Columbia University, Bureau of Publications, 1959.

132   The Nature of Dance

RUST, F. *Dance in Society*, London: Routledge & Kegan Paul, 1969.

SACHS, C. *World History of the Dance*, trans. B. Schönberg, New York: W. W. Norton & Co., 1937 (orig. publ. 1933).

SACHS, C. *Rhythm and Tempo; A Study in Music History*, New York: W. W. Norton & Co., Inc., 1953.

SAMDACH, C. V. T. *Danses Cambodgiennes*, Hanoi: Imprimerie d'Extrême Orient, 1930.

SAXENA, S. K. "The Role of Rhythm in Kathak," *Marg*, Vol. XII, no. 4, p. 48–531, Bombay, 1959.

SAYGUN, A. A. "Des danses d'Anatolie et de leur caractère rituel," *Journal International Folk Music Council*, Vol. II, p. 10–14, Cambridge, 1950.

SCHEBESTA, P. *Bei den Urwaldzwergen von Malaya*, Leipzig: Brockhaus, 1927.

SCHEBESTA, P. *Die Bambuti; Pygmäen vom Ituri*, Brussels: Inst. Roy. Col., 1938.

SCHELLONG, O. "Musik und Tanz der Papuas," *Globus*, Vol. IV, no. 6, Braunschweig, 1889.

SCHIKOWSKI, J. *Geschichte des Tanzes*, Berlin: Buchmeister-Verlag, 1926.

SCHMITZ, C. A. *Balam: Der Tanz- und Kultplatz in Melanesien als Versammlungsort und Mimischer Schauplatz*, Emsdetten: Verlag Lechte, 1955.

SCHNEIDER, M. *La danza de espadas y la tarantela*, Barcelona: Instituto español de musicologia, 1948.

SCHOCKIUS, M. *Fabula Hamelensis sive Disquisitio Historica de infausto Exitu Puerorum Hamelensium*, Groningae, 1662.

SCHOLES, P. A. *The Oxford Companion to Music*, Oxford University Press, 10th ed., 1970.

SCHRAMM, W. Ludowe obrzędy weselne we wsiach doliny Hoczewki i Tarnáwki Ziemi Sanockiej, Wrocław: PTL, 1958.

SCHURTZ, H. *Urgeschichte der Kultur*, Leipzig und Wien: Bibliographisches Institut, 1900.

SCHWANGART, F. "Tierpsychologie," *Forschungen und Fortschritte*, Vol. XX, p. 85–93, Berlin, 1944.

SELENKA, E. and L. *Sonnige Welten*, Wiesbaden, 1905.

SELER, E. *Fray Bernardino de Sahagun; Einige Kapitel aus seinem Geschichtswerk aus dem Aztekischen*, Stuttgart, 1927.

SELIGMANN, C. G. and B. Z. *The Veddas*, Cambridge University Press, 1911.

SHANIN, T. ed., *Peasants and Peasant Societies*, Harmondsworth: Penguin Books, 1971.

SHARP, C. *The Dance*, London: Halton, Truscott Smith, 1924.

SHAWN, T. *Every Little Movement*, New York: Dance Horizons, republ. from 1963 ed. (first publ. 1954).

SHEETS, M. *The Phenomenology of Dance*, Madison and Milwaukee: University of Wisconsin Press, 1966.

SIEROSZEWSKI, W. "Du chamanisme d'après les croyances des Yakoutes," *Revue de l'histoire des religions*, Vol. XLVI, Paris, 1902.

SIRE, *L'Intelligence des Animaux*, Paris, Hachette, 1954.

SKOVRAN, O., MLADENOVIĆ, O. "Problèmes et méthodes de l'adaptation scénique des danses populaires," *Journal International Folk Music Council*, Vol. VIII, p. 41–45, Cambridge, 1956.

SMITH, A. *Essays on Philosophical Subjects*, London: Cadell & Davies, 1795.

SOBIESCY, J. and M. "Tempo rubato u Chopina i w polskiej muzyce ludowej," *Muzyka*, no. 3, Warsaw, 1960.

SOBOLEWSKA-DRABECKA, M. "Niektóre zagadnienia z najdawniejszych dziejów tańca," *Swiatowit*, Vol. XXIII, p. 87–112, Warsaw, 1960.

SOLARI, M. L. "Notation de la Danza," *Revista Musical Chilena*, Vol. XII, no. 58, p. 42–58, Santiago, 1958.

SOURIAU, E. *La Correspondance des Arts*, Paris: Flammarion, 1947.

SPENCE, L. *Myth and Ritual in Dance, Game and Rhyme*, London: Watts & Co., 1947.

SPENCER, H. *The Principles of Psychology*, London: Longman & Co., 1855.

SPENCER, H. "Dancer and Musician," *Popular Science Monthly*, p. 364–74, London, July 1895.

SPENCER, H. "On the Origin of Dancing," *Spectator*, p. 12–13, London, July 1895.

STEARNS, M. W. *The Story of Jazz*, New York: Oxford University Press, Inc., 1956.

STEINER, G. *Language and Silence*, London: Faber & Faber, 1967.

STEINER, G. "The Language Animal," *Encounter*, p. 7–24, London, August, 1969.

STEINTHAL, H. *Zur Bibel und Religionsphilosophie; Vorträge und Abhandlungen*, Berlin: Neue Folge, 1895.

STELMACHOWSKA, B. *"Podkoziolek" w obrzędach zapustnych Polski Zachodniej*, Poznań: 1933.

STELMACHOWSKA, B. *Rok obrzędowy na Pomorzu*, Toruń: 1933.

STIEGELMAN, A. *Altamira*, Bonn: 1910.

STOCKMANN, D. "Der Dresdener Kongress für Tanzschrift und Volkstanzforschung," *Deutsches Jahrbuch für Volkskunde*, Vol. IV, p. 160, Berlin, 1958.

STRATOU, D. *The Greek Dances—our living link with Antiquity*, Athens: 1966.

SULIŢEANU, G. "Probleme de metodologie în culegerea şi studierea muzicii dansurilor populare din Muscel; Aplicarea metodiča,

134   The Nature of Dance

čiteva rezultate și principii metodologice," *Revista de etnografie și folclor*, Vol. X, p. 503–17, Bucharest, 1965.

SUNA, CH. "Narodnaja choreografija na prazdnikach pesni i tanca Sovetskoj Latvii," *International Congress of the Anthropological and Ethnological Sciences*, Moscow University, 1964.

ŠUŠTAR, M. *Slovenski Ljudski Plesi; Primorske*, Ljubljana: Glasbeno Narodopisni Institut, 1958.

SUTTON-SMITH, B. *The Games of New Zealand Children*, Berkeley: University of California Press, 1959.

SZENTPÁL, O. "Die Bedeutung der Kinetographie bei der Formanalyse des Volkstanzes," MS. Leipzig, Institut für Volkskunstforschung beim Zentralhaus für Volkskunst, 1957.

SZENTPÁL, O. "Versuch einer Formanalyse der ungarischen Volkstänze," *Acta Ethnographica Ac. Sc. Hungaricae*, Vol. VII, p. 3–4, Budapest, 1958.

TAGIROV, G. *Tatarskije tancy*, Kazan: 1960.

TAUBERT, G. *Rechtschaffener Tantzmeister*, Leipzig: Fr. Lanckischens Erben, 1717.

TAX, S., CALLENDER, C. (eds.) *Evolution After Darwin; The University of Chicago Centennial*, Chicago University Press, 1960.

THALBITZER, W. "Cultic Games and Festivals in Greenland," *Congrès International des Américanistes, Compte-Rendu de la XXIe session*, p. 236-55, Göteborg, 1925.

THURNWALD, R. *Psychologie des primitiven Menschen*, Munich: 1922.

THURSTON, H. A. "What is a Folk Dance," *The Folklorist*, Vol. VI, no. 2, Manchester, 1960.

TIMAŠEVA, L. *Tancy narodov Severa*, Magadan: 1959.

TOGI, M. *Gagaku; Court Music and Dance*, New York, Tokyo and Kyoto: Weatherhill, 1971.

TOITA, Y. *Kabuki; The Popular Theater*, New York, Tokyo and Kyoto: Weatherhill, 1970.

TOPITSCH, E. VON, *Ursprung und Ende der Methaphysik*, Vienna: Springer, 1958.

TOPITSCH, E. VON, "Phylogenetische und Emotionelle Grundlagen Menschlicher Weltauffassung," *Kulturanthropologie*, Mühlmann and Müller, Köln-Berlin: Verlag Kiepenheuer & Witsch, 1966 (orig. publ. 1962).

TOSCHI, P. "A Question about the Tarantella," *Journal International Folk Music Council*, Vol. II, p. 19, Cambridge, 1950.

TRIPP, E. *The Handbook of Classical Mythology*, London: Arthur Barker Ltd., 1970.

TYLOR, E. B. *Primitive Culture*, London: J. Murray, 1871.

TYLOR, E. B. *Anthropology*, London: Macmillan & Co., 1881.

VALÉRY, P. *L'Âme et la Danse*, Paris: Librairie Gallimard, 1923.

VALÉRY, P. *Degas. Danse. Dessin.*, Paris: Libraire Gallimard, 1938.

VATSYAYAN, K. "Notes on the Relationship of Music and Dance in India," *Ethnomusicology*, Vol. VII, no. 1. p. 33–38, Middletown, 1963.

VERGER, P. *Les Dieux d'Afrique*, Paris: P. Hartmann, 1954.

WILLETARD, H. "La Danse ecclésiastique à la Métropole de Sens," *Bull. de la Soc. Archéol. de Sens*, Vol. XXVI, p.. 105, Sens, 1911.

VOBLOV, I. K. "Eskimosskije prazdniki," *Sibirskij etnografičeskij sbornik*, Vol. I, Moscow and Leningrad, 1952.

VORE, I. DE, ed. *Primate Behaviour*, New York: Holt, Rinehart and Winston, 1965.

VUIA, R. "The Rumanian Hobby-Horse, the Căluşari," *Journal of the English Folk Dance and Song Society*, Vol. II, London, 1935.

WAHL, M. *Le Mouvement dans la Peinture*, Paris: F. Alcan, 1936.

WALLASCHEK, R. *Primitive Music*, London and New York: Longmans Green, 1893.

WAVELL, S., BUTT, A., EPTON, N. *Trances*, London: George Allen & Unwin, 1966.

WEBSTER, H. *Primitive Secret Societies*, New York: Macmillan & Co., 1908.

WENZEL, M. "Graveside Feasts and Dances in Yugoslavia," *Folk Lore*, Vol. LXXIII, p. 1–12, London, 1962.

WERNER, H. *Einführung in die Entwicklungspsychologie*, Leipzig: J. A. Barth, 1926.

WETTER, G. "La Danse rituelle dans l'Eglise ancienne," *Revue d'histoire et de Litt. relig.*, Vol. VIII, p. 254, Paris, 1922.

WICKE, E. C. *Versuch einer Monographie des grossen Veitstanzes und der unwillkülichen Muskelbewegungen, nebst Bemerkungen über den Taranteltanz und die Beriberi*, Leipzig: 1844.

WIORA, W. "La Musique à l'Epoque de la Peinture Paléolithique," *Journal International Folk Music Council*, Vol. XIV, p. 1–6, Cambridge, 1962.

WIRZ, P. *Dämonen und Wilde in Neuguinea*, Stuttgart: Strecker & Schröder, 1928.

WITKOWSKI, L. "Einige Bemerkungen über den Veitstanz des Mittelalters und über psychische Infection," *Allgemeine Zeitschrift für Psychiatrie*, Vol. 35, p. 591, Berlin, 1879.

WITZIG, L. "Nordisches Volkstanztreffen in Helsingfors 7.–10. Juli 1950," *Heimatleben*, Vol. XXIV, no. 1–2, Zürich, 1951.

WOLFRAM, R. "European Song-Dance Forms," *Journal International Folk Music Council*, Vol. VIII, p. 32–36, Cambridge, 1956.

WOLFRAM, R. "Der Volkstanz als kulturelle Ausdrucksform der Süd-Europäischen Völker," *Die Volkskultur der südeuropäischen Völker*, Munich: 1962.

WOOD, M. *Advanced Historical Dances*, London: C. W. Beaumont, 1960.

WOODS, J. D. ed., *The Native Tribes of South Australia*, Adelaide: Wigg, 1879.

WUNDT, W. *Völkerpsychologie*, Stuttgart and Leipzig: 1900–21.

WYNNE-EDWARDS, V. C. *Animal Dispersion in Relation to Social Behaviour*, Edinburgh and London: Oliver & Boyd, 1962.

YANG, H. and G. (trans.), *The Fisherman's Revenge (A Peking Opera)*, Peking: Foreign Languages Press, 1956.

ZOETE, B. DE, SPIES, W. *Dance and Drama in Bali*, London: Faber and Faber Ltd., 1938.

ZOETE, B. DE, *Dance and Magic Drama in Ceylon*, London: Faber and Faber Ltd., 1957.

ŽORNICKAJA, M. J. "Narodnyje tancy Evenov i Evenkov Jakutskoj ASSR," *Sovetskaja etnografija*, no. 2, p. 116–122, Moscow, 1964.

ŽORNICKAJA, M. J. *Narodnyje tancy Jakutii*, Moscow: Nauka, 1966.

INDEX

138 *Index*